HIS HEALING HANDS

Warren Frankel, M.D.

CHRISTIAN GROWTH
PUBLISHERS INC®

His Healing Hands

ISBN 978-0-940445-30-7

Published by
Christian Growth Publishers, Inc
P. O. Box 999
Atascadero, CA 93423

Printed in the United States of America

Cover and book design by
Maurice T. Wagner
MTGraphics

08 09 10 11

He became like us so
we could become like Him.

INTRODUCTION

This Book is a travel log, an adventure, a missionary journey, a philosophical treatise and a spiritual pathway to fill an emptiness of the heart. But most of all, it is an autobiography of a Jewish New York medical doctor who asks God to reveal himself to him and in the process finds the God of the universe.

Since childhood, I have thought about death, triggered by the death of my father when I was only eight years old. I wanted to understand who I was, where I had come from, where I was going, and where I would eventually end up in eternity.

The Old Testament of my people gave me some answers, but when I shut off the light at night, in my bed, I was all alone with a terrible empty feeling inside as if something was missing. I was afraid of the last unknown frontier; death.

I was challenged to read the New Testament; the Gentile Bible. I had to decide, who was this Jesus of Nazareth? Was He a religious fanatic, a good teacher, a philosopher, a prophet, a lunatic, or was he the Jewish Messiah who He said He was; The God of Abraham, Isaac, and Jacob.

I read the book of Matthew and was shocked to discover a document written in the same style and openness as the Jewish scriptures, and not at all anti-Semitic as I had been warned.

I prayed that God would reveal himself to me as instructed by the Jewish Bible; The Old Testament. I prayed this prayer with an open heart and mind. I came to the startling conclusion, If Jesus was the God of Abraham, Isaac, and Jacob and the Jewish Messiah, that we are all waiting for, then in order to remain Jewish I had to accept Him as my Lord and Savior. I realized that the most Jewish thing that I would ever do, was to accept the Jewish Messiah.

God revealed Himself to me and all I had to do was to ask Him to open my heart.

I had been spiritually blind and the veil over my eyes had been lifted by His Healing Hands.

Maybe after reading my story, you will also open your heart to a new relationship with the God of the universe.

Warren Frankel

TABLE OF CONTENTS

CHAPTER ONE
"Doctor Livingston, I Presume" 1

CHAPTER TWO
I Made A Deal with God. 13

CHAPTER THREE
Gypsies, Tramps, and Thieves 25

CHAPTER FOUR
Ambivalence About Vietnam 41

CHAPTER FIVE
We Died On An Indian Highway 53

CHAPTER SIX
The Providence of God 67

CHAPTER SEVEN
Christianity is not a Religion but an Intimate Relationship 77

CHAPTER EIGHT
God Raises up Workers for the Harvest 89

CHAPTER NINE
There is Not Enough Time in a Day But God Will Redeem the Time . 99

CHAPTER TEN
Christmas in a City Dump 107

Table of Contents

CHAPTER ELEVEN
Dodge City of the Old West in Kenya 113

CHAPTER TWELVE
It is Better to be Given the Tools to Fish - Than to be Given Fish 127

CHAPTER THIRTEEN
Has Anyone Seen Osama?. 139

CHAPTER FORTEEN
You Meant It for Harm But God Meant It For Good 149

CHAPTER FIFTEEN
"A Prophet is Never Recognized in His Own Town". 159

CHAPTER SIXTEEN
"His Healing Hands" 169

CHAPTER SEVENTEEN
We Have not forgotten to Serve Our People At Home 175

CHAPTER EIGHTEEN
Can You Handle The Truth?. 187

CHAPTER NINETEEN
Conclusion / Beginnings 191

CHAPTER TWENTY
"My Grace Is Sufficient For Thee" - Epilogue. 199

Lake Tanganyika, a refreshing surprise on the western boarder of Tanzania

"Doctor Livingston, I Presume"

Standing on a hillside overlooking pristine Lake Tanganyika in Kigoma Tanzania, across from Rwanda and the Congo, I knew that I had returned to a familiar place. This was not possible, as it was my first trip to Africa. I had never been in Tanzania and yet this scene before my eyes was recognizable and comfortably familiar and pleasant to my memory. I just wrote it off, as Yogi Berra would say

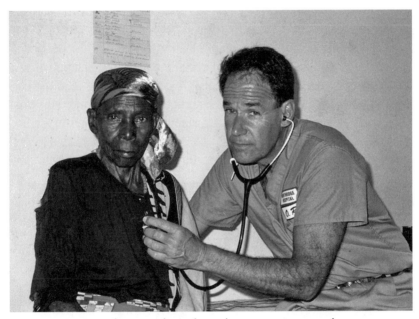

Typical patient in Kigoma, Tanzania

"déjà vu all over again" and one of the many strange feelings in life. But it haunted me and I would later realize that it involved the early years of my growing up in New York City.

My life has been a series of apparent contradictions: a New York City street person living on a ranch and vineyard in central California, a medical doctor in solo practice farming pistachio nuts and growing wine grapes, a medical missionary participating in medical humanitarian aid around the world, an orthodox Jew who believes Jesus is the Messiah, and a third generation part Polish, Russian, Hungarian, Austrian immigrant living in the wealthiest country in the world going to Kigoma, Tanzania treating the poorest, most wretched, malnourished Islamic people of Southeast Africa. These people have malaria, typhoid fever, aids, worms, and liver flukes, combined with extreme poverty, filth, heat, humidity, superstitions and lack of fresh water. The sanitary conditions are non-existent, exacerbated by cultural uncleanliness, in addition to acquiring the routine diseases of all other cultures. When you research diseases of the world related to geography, South Eastern Africa always has the most virulent, active, contagious, communicable diseases of the entire world. How did I arrive in this place in my life?

In 1944, New York City was not only a great place to be from, but it was a wonderful place to live and grow up on the streets. When I was born on the lower east side of Manhattan Island, the country was in high gear with hope and aspirations on the upswing. The tide of war was changing, the economy was going to see better days, and the parents in our country wanted something better for their children. What they meant by better was economic stability with unlimited hope and freedom to pursue their own ideas and values. These industrious second generation Americans had just been through a depression and a dev-

Young African children, watching the Jesus film in their own language in a remote jungle location in Tanzania.

astating world war and were yearning for peace and permanence. They were willing to work hard to achieve the "American dream." Hope and aspirations are essential for an emerging national power, because without a vision, the nation will eventually fade away and die. Our country had a worthwhile cause, a purpose, a mission to free the world from fascism and to win freedom for its children even at the cost of self-denial and sacrifice. Hard work and a job were considered a blessing and fighting for

A beautiful African woman

ideals was admired. Escaping from fear and achieving the "good" life was seen as the rewards for future generations. Our generation is the recipient of those hard driving, goal oriented, idealistic Americans, and we have reaped the benefits of what they have sowed.

In 1944, my family consisted of my 28-year-old mother, a seamstress, my 30-year-old father, a window cleaner, and my 4-year-old sister. We lived on 15th street and avenue A, in a 80 year old tenement on the lower east side of New York City in Manhattan on the border of little Italy, Chinatown and a self-imposed Jewish ghetto. My father cleaned windows of tall buildings with his brother and father. They were hard working and industrious, but I have to laugh. When I first came to California as a surgical intern, my California cousin asked me with hesitation and trepidation, "Are you a window cleaner like the rest of your laboring uneducated family?" I'm not a window cleaner but if I had been, I would have been a millionaire and she wouldn't have asked the question. When I was 8 years old, my father died of multiple sclerosis after a long protracted period of being bed-ridden. My

My Daughter Faith giving her Bible to Juma, our guide in the jungle in Tanzania

mother supported my sister and me, as best she could, by sewing, and collecting unemployment insurance when no work was available. She paid the rent and kept food on the table, but as a result, I was left to my own devices on the streets of New York at the early age of 3 years old. Today, we tell our children not to speak to strangers. I loved and needed strangers. I lived on the third floor of an apartment building and couldn't reach the third floor button in the elevator. I was delighted to see any stranger to push the button for me. It was a different era with different values. I loved to talk to adults in the elevator and they gave me their pearls of wisdom for the day. One diminutive, round, elderly Italian lady would see me almost everyday and would give me the same advise day after day in her broken English with a thick Italian accent as if she had never counseled me previously. She told me that my name was my most important possession. Daily, she instructed me, that a good name must be developed, guarded and prized, as it would follow me all my life. She told me this at age three and continued until I left that apartment to be on my own at age twenty-one. In fact, I would see her occasionally after that time when I visited my mother and that wonderful little woman gave me the same advise with the same enthusiasm as if for the first time. In the forties and fifties in New York City, people were part of neighborhoods and looked after each other. I was never lonely and acquaintances on the street seemed to care for me and I felt very comfortable and very much at home.

It was a time of change, where horse-drawn pushcarts, and trucks shared the same streets. There were stables next to electronic stores with the new invention called television. Growing up on the streets of New York in the forties and fifties was glorious. The sounds and smells of the sidewalks were an intriguing playground for any American kid. I loved it. I went to public school during the day and hung out with my gang member friends at night in the local pool hall or the bowling alley. Although my mother worried about me, she was too busy supporting us to control an eight year old without a father figure. My sister was four years older than me and was busy with her own life, and so I had a free reign of the streets of the city. Jews, especially New York Jews are goal oriented, self-sufficient, education-loving people. I was "saved" by my Jewish traditions of education.

I went to public school 61, junior high school 104, Stuyvesant High School, Brooklyn College, and Albert Einstein medical school. But I loved the streets, the gangs, the camaraderie of Italian Americans in little Italy, the music of the Apollo theater in Harlem, my Asian friends in Chinatown and the Jews of the lower east side. I had a goal. I was going to cure multiple sclerosis and save the world. My street friends teased me about going to school and studying and not being a tough street person, like them. In the late nineteen seven-

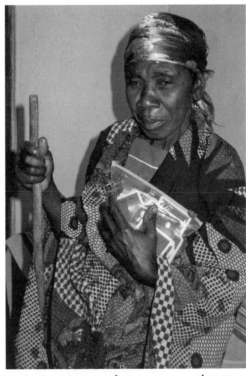

Elderly Tanzanian woman tightly holding her medicines

Wendy Scalise, the former mayor of Atascadero,
California, lining up children for a medical clinic in
Bigabiru, Tanzania.

ties, when I went back to Manhattan to see my old friends, they ostra-cized me for leaving New York and "becoming somebody," a regular citizen. Some of my friends had died, others were in jail, and the ones remaining, became the local bookmakers or were involved with the Mafia or became store owners. I still love to watch movies about New York, like the Dead End Kids or the Mafia or any period piece about the city that never sleeps.

My wife says that my life is an imitation of every "B" movie I've ever seen. It's not true. I've only incorporated "A" movies into my life: "Here's looking at you kid," "Tomorrow is another day," "We had him when He decided to be somebody," "May the force be with you," "Doctor Livingston I presume." Which explains why I recognized Lake Tanganyika in Africa.

In the early nineteen fifties, television was just beginning. I loved to come home from school and watch all the old movies with my invalid father who was unable to walk but could share his experiences with me. One of my favorite movies was "Stanley and Livingston," with Spencer Tracy and Sir Cedric Hardwick. It was a story of an American reporter looking for an English medical missionary in deep dark Africa, who was helping the poor natives without thought to himself. My father had been sick for all the years of my young life and when a doctor came to my house, that physician was revered. My fate was sealed, but Dr. Livingston was a Christian medical missionary and I was an orthodox Jew. How could I emulate my hero? I also liked Humphrey Bogart, especially in "Casablanca" and "African Queen." Bogart's characters always had bigger, more important causes then their own little lives, which "aren't worth a hill of beans compared to the cause." I guess my life is definitely a conglomeration of old movies.

I stood on that hilltop in Kigoma, Tanzania, and I felt at home. It was oh so familiar. It was very strange. I was in Kigoma, Tanzania to do medical missionary work in a church in Bigabiru, Tanzania. Kigoma was almost exactly halfway around the world from my small hometown in California, U.S.A. We had driven four hours to the Los Angeles airport, and then boarded a ten-hour flight to London, followed by a six-hour layover, followed by another ten-hour flight to Nairobi, Kenya, another one-hour layover, and finally a one-hour flight to Dar Salaam, Tanzania. We stayed in a hotel in Dar Salaam and had dinner with our Tanzanian hosts. The next morning we took a small puddle-jumper twin engine prop-plane on a three-hour trek all across the width of Tanzania. We flew over the African plain above unspoiled territory untouched since

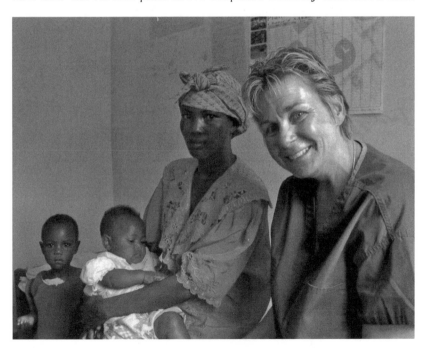

Janet Hedges, RN, treating a family in Ujiji, Tanznia

*A packed church service, standing room only
in Kigoma, Tanzania*

the time of Dr. Livingston. At our dinner in Dar Salaam, I sat next to a Tanzanian doctor, who told me how she admired us for going to Kigoma, because even she and her colleagues wouldn't go there, and they were her own people and she spoke Swahili. That was the exact reason we had decided to go to this extremely remote region. No one would go there and many of these people had never seen a medical doctor and had never experienced the love of God through His people. We saw hundreds of poor people every day, and gave out thousands of medicines. We had an endless supply of patients and they expressed their gratitude on their faces. We were exhausted. Then, that first evening, a Christian missionary, named Lowell Wertz of "Joy in the Harvest," came to our hotel after hearing about our medical clinic. He offered to take us out on his fishing boat on Lake Tanganyika, just down the road, out of Ujiji. We were tired but this was Africa and we couldn't resist. He told us that the movie "African Queen" had been filmed on Lake Tanganyika and the German steamship Luisa, blown up in the movie, was still docked on the lake. We sailed by the Luisa. He then recited the history of Kigoma. He described how Morton Stanley hunted for Dr. Livingston for two years across Africa, and found him in the town of Ujiji, down the road from Kigoma on the lake.

Some people believe in fate, some believe in chance plus time, or just maybe there is an all-knowing, all-powerful, prime mover who organizes and can influence all human behavior. It was both very strange and very real to me. This scene of Lake Tanganyika was embedded in my mind for over forty-five years from the movies I had watched with my father. This movie had made an impression on me for all these years. Now, I was living a life like that Christian medical missionary "lost" in Africa, but it appears as if I was "found" by God and used in a way that is bigger than myself.

The movie "Stanley and Livingston," affected me and sealed my desire to be a doctor but added a notion, which I thought at the time was just a romantic idea to help the needy and the poor in deepest, dark Africa. Bogart, in the movie "African Queen," was risking his life to fight against tyranny in his own little way, doing what was at least available to him at the time. These movies stamped on my brain, like a baby chick is imprinted to follow his mother, even a mother that looks and acts differently than what was expected. Standing on that hilltop over Lake Tanganyika, I felt like the ugly duckling that had finally found his place on earth. A puzzle piece that fits just right.

How does a New York Jewish street person become a Christian medical missionary traveling with a non-profit, non-denominational organization called "His Healing Hands?" How does he go all over the world to Haiti, China, Tanzania, Kenya, Vietnam, India, Belize, Mexico, Indonesia (after the tsunami), and Pakistan (after a killer earthquake), to heal, teach and preach in the name of Jesus? Maybe it is just happenstance or could it be God's plan? It is not my intention to argue or persuade anyone concerning my point of view or my belief system. It is my personal account of what I have seen and heard and the events in my life as they occurred. It is my witness but the conclusions are up to you, the reader.

In deciding to write this book, I hesitated because I figured I had to do a great deal of research like Haley did in "Roots," to make this an accurate, factual account. However, because of my inertia or the lack of desire to perform exhaustive research and not wanting to hate the writing of this book, I decided not to clutter this account with researched facts and accurateness. I wanted to enjoy the writing. Everything I have written is my own impression and my own opinions and view of events as I remembered them. It is events, filtered through my mind based on my personal perceptions. In it's inaccuracy, it is the most accurate account a mind can retell. It is events and ideas as I experienced them and not as chronicled by someone else. This entire paragraph, should really be placed in the preface, but since I have never read the preface in any book, why should you?

There is an age-old debate of whether it is nature or nurture that creates our personality and dictates the path we take in life. Previously, I thought that my life was directed only by me but now I have my doubts. There seems to be a guidance system that is apart from me; a prime mover; an intelligent entity. When looking back at my life, there are incidences and directions that had a direct bearing on my growth and development that appeared to be beyond my control or desires at the time. In hindsight, my path has been directed by His healing hands. I will never forget that night on Lake Tanganyika when for the first time, my life made sense. In my youth, the trials and tribulations that I went through while growing up in New York City now seemed to be placed in perspective. Without my awareness I was being guided by the providence of God.

Nile Pike caught in Lake Tanganyika

Jometre, my Haitian translator, who "adopted" me as his
father in Port-au-Prince, Haiti.

I Made A Deal with God

I can still smell the horses in the stalls on 10th street and Ave B in the livery stable on the lower east side of Manhattan, and the sounds and the sweet odor of the garbage trucks dumping their refuse off the pier at 22nd street into the East River. I have experienced those sounds and smells many times since I was a boy growing up in New York City. The noise of the garbage trucks and the pungent odors of refuse in Port-Au- Prince, Haiti, the garbage dumps of Vietnam, and the trash heaps of Belize and Romania where I treated patients who lived in these garbage hovels as the literal refuse of their cities, brought me back to my youth in New York.

The happiest recollections of my childhood in New York were playing stoopball in back alleyways, reading superman comic books, and playing stickball. I had hoped to hit two sewers, imitating my hero Willie Mays, the only three-sewer man that ever played stickball on the streets of New York. I remember going to bed Sunday night and watching the snow fall and hoping it would snow enough to close school Monday morning. When this happened, the white quiet streets were beautiful, unspoiled by the gray slush of mud and gasoline, and without the belching smoke of busses, honking taxis, or rushing people going hurriedly to work. If this did occur, I would dress warmly, take a subway ride to the Bronx Zoo and watch the polar bears frolicking in the snow and batting around snowflakes. I was alone with the animals in the calm, clear, crisp, air of a miraculously magnificent day. That calmness is a far cry from the horrible, filthy, overcrowded, disease infested, hot, humid, mosquito plagued, squalor of Haiti; my first exposure to medical missionary work. I went with a team from Northwest Medical Teams out of Portland, Oregon. I had been looking for a humanitarian experience, as I needed a psychological lift in my medical career. They were the only group that was willing to take me with them on short notice. I later realized that they wanted me because no one else was willing to go to Haiti and I soon found out the reason. My father-in-law, who spent two years in the navy during World War Two, told me never to volunteer for anything. But God's sacrificial love, called agape love is not judgmental or prejudicial and it doesn't wait for an invitation, it volunteers. I volunteered.

Haiti is the poorest country in the western hemisphere and has the reputation of being the vilest place on the planet. The national religion of Haiti is Voodoo. The people of Haiti appeared to hate white people as they yelled expletives at us and called us Blanco (whites). There is no sanitation, and the weather is hot, sticky, and humid, with stifling smoldering smog making the air almost unbreathable. There is garbage everywhere, being scavenged by wondering dogs and goats, with the populace spilling over onto the streets and waste running down the sidewalks where the children play. When it rains, it doesn't wash the air clean and all the debris starts to come at you down the streets. When we were there, the government was apparently democratic but the soldiers all carried automatic weapons and would shoot people on the streets including children for what seemed to be no apparent reason.

We stayed in an orphanage set up by a Christian missionary named "Mom" Workman. She had felt the calling of God while living in California. This blessed black woman came to Haiti by herself and started an orphanage with the children of "boat" people who lost their lives at sea while trying to escape from Haiti. Their over-crowded boat with fifteen hundred adults, sank off the coast of Haiti in view of the shore. These parents were seeking freedom from oppression. They were planning to send for their children once they were established in the United States. These fifteen hundred parents died and left thousands of orphans in Haiti.

Eleanor Workman took these children off the streets. She also went to the pediatric wards of the local hospitals in Port-Au-Prince and asked for the most hopeless cases to care for them in her makeshift orphanage. When I was there, she spoke at a church service and told us about one baby that was born without a bony spine or spinal cord. She was told that the baby would never see, hear, and of course never talk or walk or be able to move at all. She cared for this baby and all the others and prayed. She told God: "You called me for this work and gave me these babies and now you have to uphold me and enable me to care for these, your children." She is a very bold woman who relies on God's promises and feels comfortable going before God with her righteous intrepid requests. She then turned around and asked the drummer behind her in the band on stage to stand. Her prayer was twenty years ago and this healthy, active twenty-year-old drummer was the baby without a spine that she asked God to heal.

When, I first decided to do medical missionary work, I made a "deal" with God. I am a Jewish believer. That means, as a Jew, I believe in the God of Abraham, Isaac, and Jacob and the truth and the prophesies of the Jewish Bible, the "Old" Testament. I also believe that the Messiah, that all Bible based Jews are awaiting, is none other than Jesus, the Galilean, born in Nazareth of the line of King David. We, Jews are of Mediterranean descent and in the true Semitic tradition make "deals." I don't mean to be arrogant or sacrilegious with regard to my

Piled up garbage on a sidewalk of a typical Haitian street.

personal relationship to God, or demeaning to my people. This was the "deal," I requested. I would go on these medical trips to the most under-privileged needy areas of the world and in return, I wanted God to give me more faith. The Bible says all good things come from above, even our faith. I wanted more faith, so I could step out in that faith, and be bold for God, as exemplified by "Mom" Workman. I have seen men and women of God who are bolder for God and risk more for God without fear or apprehension than I would ever risk. I have been in the company of truly brave men and women. I now understand that it is not bravery; it is faith. Many of my colleague's say I am brave, to go to the undeveloped countries with our organization, "His Healing Hands." Fear can be paralyzing and will prevent us from accomplishing what we want to achieve. I now believe that for me it's not bravery, it is faith. If I have the faith that God is in control, then all I have to do, is let God be on the throne of my life and then "step" down from the control reigns, in faith, then all fear will melt away. That's what I wanted and I knew that if I stepped out more, in faith, then I would develop more faith and step out even more. This would keep feeding on itself, resulting in my being a more mature, bold, and sanctified man of God. It sounds as if I am giving up my freedom and independence. In reality, I am freer

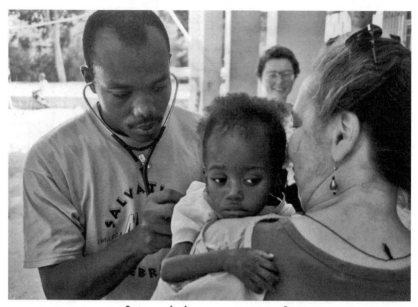

Dr. Franco, one of the original orphans of "Mom" Workman examining an orphan in a Mariana Haitian orphanage.

than I have ever been. My desire is to serve God out of gratefulness for what God has done for me. He has loved me, and demonstrated that love by creating me and dying for me without my deserving this un-merited grace and favor. It was said by a little boy "God does not make junk." Our lives are worthwhile and we should have a good self-image because we are God's creation and He demonstrated our value to Him by suffering for us. I am grateful. I am not trying to repay God, which I can never do. What can anyone offer God? God owns it all and He has created everything. When someone does something for my loved ones, or me, I am grateful and appreciative. It creates in me a natural and compelling desire to please them; not out of guilt or duty but out of joy and desire. There is another issue. It is self-denial, which is not un-derstood by non-Christians and misused by many other Christians. My early childhood hero David Livingston, the English pioneer missionary to Africa, when asked about his lifelong denial of himself, he replied, "People talk of the sacrifice I have made in spending so much of my life in Africa. Can that be called a sacrifice, which brings its own best reward in healthful activity, the consciousness of doing good, peace of mind, and the bright hope of a glorious hereafter? I never made a sacrifice!" My desire to serve is based solely on gratitude and thanksgiving. It is a delight to serve God and His people and not a duty. It is a blessing not a burden and this opportunity is not an obligation. It is my privilege and honor. Only with that attitude will I be able to help others with joy and gladness.

I want to demonstrate the love of God through my medical missionary endeavors, solely out of appreciation and not trying to work my way to heaven. There is the story of a family asleep at night in their home, when a fire starts in their basement. The fire department responds and one of the firemen repeatedly goes in and out of the burning building, carrying out two young children and their two coughing, smoke inhaled, overcome parents. The entire family is saved and in the process the fireman receives multiple second-degree burns. The family asks if they can help the fireman and his family, not for themselves as they are already saved but out of gratefulness for what he has done. Their desire to help is out of gratitude. I am grateful to God for so many things, not the least of which is His paying the price for me eternally. This is service based on gratitude and not guilt.

These medical trips have definitely increased my faith and have brought me more joy in my life than anything I have ever done or experienced. It is on par with the joy I have from my wife and children. The writing of this book stems from my desire to share this joy with anyone that is opened enough to accept it. Again, I am not trying to convince or proselytize but to write what I've experienced and seen and heard. This disclaimer has been repetitious but it is very important for every man or woman to make up their own mind concerning their relationship to God and their fellow men. After all, what can be more important?

The first night I spent in Haiti, sleeping on the floor of the orphanage, I was uncomfortable, anxious, and totally self-consumed. I remember thinking to myself while lying on that dirt floor, that I had survived one night and only had eleven days to go. I would "guts it out." What an attitude to serve people. Where was the joy? Where was the love? Where was the peace? I had to do something. I prayed that entire sleepless night that God would change my outlook. I was the only doctor in our medical group and I was worried about getting malaria and not being able to function and thereby letting everyone down. It was still about me. That night, I could feel mosquitoes attacking me continuously. God must have answered my prayer as I finally fell into a very restful, relaxing sleep with a renewed desire to serve and enjoy these Haitian people. When I awoke, the mosquitoes that I had felt were in reality ants that had been crawling on me. I was relieved and ready to rally the troops and excitedly treat these wonderful, grateful, needy people. My focus had been altered by God through prayer, and my focus helped me to determine my reality. Haiti in many ways is a very evil place, but people are the same all over the world, and if you help them in love, they are appreciative, thoughtful and loving in return. William Blake said, "The eye that alters, alters all." My eye, my vision, my attitudes were being altered by focusing on God's people, and trying to view them from God's perspective.

We spent a delightful two weeks treating all the people brought to us and their appreciative words and faces were all the reward anyone would ever want. I was captivated and I knew that I had found my place and position in the world. It was possibly, the first time that I had truly forgotten about myself and focused on other peoples needs and serving God. This was an unbelievable feeling. I knew that I was in the right place at the right time. This "feeling," I have subsequently learned is living in the will of God. It has since occurred in my life several times but strangely enough, it usually happens on the mission field. Possibly, because that is when I am focusing on God and his created children and not on myself. It seems that living the American success story was really not about caring about myself and my every need. In the long run, that is not satisfying or fulfilling. Americans have always helped the needy, which is what has made our country and our people great.

I remember treating one young man in a clinic we had set up outside the orphanage, literally on the streets of Port-Au-Prince. He had multiple abscesses all over his body. I drained a few of these pus–ladened lesions and gave him intramuscular Rocephin, a strong antibiotic. Everyday we had him return for more I and D's (incision and drainage) and another injection but he kept developing new abscesses. I finally checked his blood sugar and discovered he was a diabetic giving himself injections of insulin with unsterile reusable needles. He had been injecting himself with bacteria and creating these abscesses. We took his needles away and eventually this man started to heal all his infected areas and we were able to stabilize his diabetes on oral hypoglycemic agents, eliminating the risks of these unsterile needles. I had started to learn about the unusual disease states that I would find in third world nations. We have the ability and knowledge of modern medicine, but these are not available to these people. I have been a medical doctor for thirty-five years and I was starting to rely on my old, tried and true, sometimes antiquated methods, since modern techniques were not available on the streets of these third world nations. It was as if,

Baptismal service in a Haitian river. Later we learned that there were alligators down stream

my entire life was leading up to these medical missionary endeavors. My life as a child on the streets of New York City had prepared me to love poor street people and be comfortable with them. My education in a melting pot of cultures had made the diversity of ethnicity irresistible to me. My medical training had enabled me to offer these people a service and fulfill a need. However, all of my past experiences leading up to the present time could only come to fruition in a humanitarian mission, once I believed in God and wanted to serve Him.

We gave all the children of the orphanage vitamins and dewormed them and bathed them all with kwell shampoo to treat lice. The women of our team were never without a baby sitting on their laps or hanging around their necks. All children respond to physical, touching, and expressive love. One of the initial children of "Mom" Workman's orphanage twenty years ago was our medical liaison in Haiti. We worked together in Haiti and we have kept in contact for many years. He is currently teaching in the University Of Miami as an infectious disease consult in their medical school. This medical doctor is only one example of the effect of "Mom" Workman's love of God and how one determined person with a godly mission could change the world for the people she contacts.

When it was time to leave Haiti, it was very difficult to separate from new friendships we had made and new patients we had treated. We became very attached to each other. We came to realize this mission trip was the honor, the opportunity and the chance to do something

Our transportation in Haiti, an old diesel dump truck

worthwhile. It represents the dignity of the human race to give of itself to help others. We had made a difference in many lives. One of my translators, who was with me constantly, for long hours, became very close to me and started calling me "daddy." In Haiti, it is not unusual for men to take common law wives and have three or four children with them and then leave the house and pick another woman. This seems to be accepted as the norm. Jometre was a product of such a union. Since I left Haiti, we have kept in touch by the internet and the telephone and my family has financially helped Jometre go to college. He has achieved a degree in business and is self-supporting. Every time, I return to Haiti, he is there to meet me and help me treat his people. These medical trips affect both the givers and the receivers, and the givers become the receivers. We get more from these trips personally then we give. God has kept up His part of "The Deal," and has increased my faith in increments as I proceed to act in trust of His care.

After my first "taste" of medical missionary work, I wanted to be more involved with this giving and the receiving of care and love. It seemed to sum up my entire career: my relationship to others, my relationship to God, my feelings about myself, and my very purpose for living. Growing up in New York City, I was faced with many crossroad types of decisions, as are all children. Where should I live? Who shall I marry? What vocation should I pursue? And generally, what do I believe and how shall I conduct my life? We never really know if our plans are right for us. I remember experiencing wonderful, exciting days in my youth but when I went to bed at night and shut off the light, I was alone. Was that all there was, or is there and should there be more? I certainly didn't understand while growing up but I understand now. Edith Schafer described, Life as a tapestry that is a tangle of threads when we look at it from the wrong side, but when we turn it over, we can see a simple, beautiful, uncomplicated picture. I now understand that we ask the wrong questions and therefore our answers never satisfy us. It is really not important where we live or what vocation we choose but who do we serve? Do we serve ourselves, which never creates a lasting satisfaction, or do we serve God, which always results in unending, permanent joy and contentment. If you agree and accept this statement then many relevant new questions arise. How do I serve God? What service suits me? And how do I start?

The last question is the easiest to answer and the hardest to accomplish. You start to serve God by deciding to do it and start now. It's a decision and an action. In my capacity as co-founder of "His Healing Hands," a medical humanitarian organization, I speak to a lot of medical personnel and ask them to join our trips. They all say the same thing. "I'd love to and some day I will go with you, but I can't go at this time. I have too many financial and family obligations and by the way how do you do it?" Simple answers always seem flippant but complicated answers are never correct. We all want to get our lives in order first and then commit to serve. It doesn't work that way with any of our

decisions. You have to choose to do it and then figure out how to accomplish your desire. Jerry Rubin, a sixties radical wrote a book called
"Do It." At least his title was correct. Once you decide to serve, all your
"excuses" will melt away. Then you need to figure out what type of
service will be appropriate for you. I chose to serve based on the place,
position and abilities in my life that God had set up for me. I am a doctor, who grew up in poverty on the streets of a big city with a love of
God and our country of freedom and unlimited opportunity. God had
prepared me to serve as a doctor to the needy people of the world.
You also have unique qualities, abilities, and distinctive talents that can
be used by God, which are "natural" to you. You don't have to become
someone else. You simply have to share your life with others. The first
question was, how do I serve God? To answer this question, you have
to know God. To find out about God, you can read His word, the Bible,
pray, and fellowship with wise biblical men and women. We all need
older, wiser, more experienced advisers in our life.

I was fatherless as a youngster with a mother occupied with at-
tempting to secure the necessities of life. I grew up on the streets with
peers as my guide. This is obviously not an ideal situation for developing
stability and maturity. This maturity can be summed up in the ability
to give and receive love. When I became a father, I was determined to
spend a lot of time with my children in order to bring them up "in the
way they should go."

In order to know "the way they should go," I had to know them
and in order to know them, I had to spent time with them. I decided to
bring them with me on many of my medical trips whenever possible.
After seeing the poverty of other countries, my children have never
complained about their rooms or any material desires. My son Luke,
who has helped me in Mexico, appreciates everything and has a great
deal of compassion for all peoples, and especially little children. My son
Paul has already been to Mexico, Belize, China, Tanzania, and Kenya by
the age of eighteen. He is currently in college and takes all of his vaca-
tions traveling with me and he tries to bring a few of his friends along.
One of his friends was working as a manager in Taco Bell, and my son
convinced him to expand his horizons and go to China on a medical
missionary trip. He isn't a Christian and knew nothing of medicine.
We taught him how to take vital signs and check the patient's blood
sugar. When he returned home, after an intense week of humanitarian

service to the Chinese peasants, he quit his job and applied to college. He is currently getting straight A's and is planning on going to medical school. This all came about because he was exposed to the love of God's people and it brought forth his own desire to love and care for people. I have tried to guide my children by the knowledge I have gained by understanding their personalities, gleaned from viewing them in many different situations. These trips have had a profound effect on them. My son Paul wants to help others and he is not materialistic and appreciates everything and everyone. My daughter Faith has gone with me to China, Tanzania, Mexico, Hungary, and Romania. She has served as my nurse and pharmacist and these experiences have led her to a medical career of her own. While, we were in Romania, we treated the most hated and mistrusted people in all of Europe, the Gypsies, who my daughter loved, and has subsequently influenced her to be a doctor to care for them in the future. We were warned not to go to the Gypsy camp, which was in the city dump. The people of Cluj, Romania told us that these Gypsies were pickpockets, thieves, and murderers, and certainly not worthy of our medical care. The citizenry of Cluj tried to frighten us and gave us cause to consider our safety. Of course, we gathered up our faith, prayed, hid our passports and valuables and headed out to the city dump of Cluj, Romania to the gypsy camp. We feared for ourselves but found needy, caring, loving family units, who were very protective of us.

The entire Gypsy camp and the "His Healing Hands" team listen to a Christian message of Salvation.

Gypsies, Tramps, and Thieves

While we were in Cluj, Romania, we worked in a local clinic with a Romanian medical staff who were delighted to be our host, because they didn't have any medicines to give their people. These patients couldn't fill their prescriptions from their local doctors because these poor people had no money for medicines and barely enough money for food. Under the previous communistic regime, the state completely cared for these people from "cradle to grave." This socialistic system, however, eliminated individual incentives and bankrupted the state. They are now a free society with a capitalistic economy. The younger generation loves the freedom and economic opportunities, but these older citizens have been caught in the transition. In our free market economy, we encourage individual initiative and our system coupled with freedom of opportunity has created a vibrant expanding economy that is the envy of the world. I believe that we need a safety net for the disabled and the extreme poor and we need to provide basic provisions for our people but we shouldn't stifle the inventiveness of our people. Communism and socialism are interesting idealistic systems but they have proven themselves not to work over and over again, and require a totalitarian dictatorship to keep its citizens in line. The Bible is specific about taking care of the poor, the orphans and the widows and we need to provide for them. It is in vogue to knock our government and our economic system as being unfair to the majority of our people. But until you see other governments and systems, you don't realize that our system based on biblical principals is the best "man can devise." These elderly Romanians were delighted to receive our free medicines. They had seen doctors, who diagnosed their conditions, and wrote prescriptions but they couldn't afford to buy the medicines. Communism and socialism had failed them and now they couldn't start all over in this new capitalistic system without provision for the elderly. They have been literally abandoned in the economic and political change-over.

In order to get to Romania, we had to arrive in Budapest, Hungary and then travel six hours through the countryside of Hungary and

Romania. The rolling hills, the fertile lands, and the Carpathian Mountains were beautiful. I met a Hungarian man on the plane who hadn't been back to Hungary since the nineteen fifty-six revolt against the Russians during the cold war. He was thrilled that American missionaries were going to Eastern Europe to help the peasant population but added that he wished we Americans would have helped fifty years ago. He wasn't bitter but said this with obvious sadness. I didn't understand and he explained that during the Hungarian revolution, they were hoping that the Americans would come to their aid. I vaguely remembered that the Eisenhower administration had declined to aid these people for fear of escalating the cold war. In the United States, our information is obtained from news bites on the radio and the television filtered through political commentary, and we don't see the people affected by our decisions. On our medical missionary adventures, we treat the poor peasants and we get the truth. "His Healing Hands" gives us the opportunity to not only help others but also to see and hear the truth, experience reality, and learn the facts about our world.

Every morning before we treated patients, George, the director of the clinic, had the staff of the clinic serve us breakfast. Sitting next to George, every morning, I noticed that George smelled like sour milk or rotted garbage. Certainly none of us mentioned this to each other, but one day we discovered that George went to the garbage dump before he arrived in the clinic. We found out that George loved the Gypsies that lived in the city dump. Every morning, he went to the dump and brought a few children to his modest home to feed them and bath them, and then returned them to the dump. George is a very humble man and would never mention this to us. After treating a few of these Gypsies in the clinic, we asked George if we could treat the Gypsies in their village. He told us that the Gypsies lived in the city dump and the citizens of Cluj avoided these hated people. George was delighted to have us go to the city dump to treat the Gypsies but he warned us. "These people have the reputation of being the thieves of Cluj and they are very distrustful of any outsiders." We came to Romania to help uncared for people and it was obvious that these people needed help. The next day, after leaving our passports, our money and the rest of our valuables in our rooms, we left for the city dump, wondering what was in store for us. When we told people in our hotel that we were going to the Gypsy camp, they were vigorous in their warnings and obvious

A Romanian home church, waiting for medical care. They all look like nesting dolls.

in their loathing for these people. We were skeptical and scared but we prayed and trusted God.

When we arrived on the outskirts of the city in a fetid, stinking, putrid mountain of garbage, George was greeted with smiles and handshakes but we were looked upon with obvious uncertainty. Their cardboard houses were "decorated" with a potpourri of discarded wallpaper, rugs, and mattresses, none of which matched. We were allowed to set up our clinic in the leader of the Gypsy' house. In fact, he was the king of the Gypsies. There were horses, pigs, and goats mixed with manure in between these hovels, along with the children picking at the mountains of refuse, looking for food and playthings. We waited for our patients but no one came to our clinic.

After waiting for about ten minutes with nobody asking for our medical care, I decided to walk down these alleyways of garbage to their homes and look inside. The Gypsy women were bathing their children in gray water. They wanted to appear presentable to us and in their best rags. They came to our clinic and we treated everyone in the village. They were the nicest, kindest most humble people we had ever treated. They gave us their best and we gave them all we had with the joy and delight of the Lord. Maybe we were treating angels in disguise. We cared for the least of these.

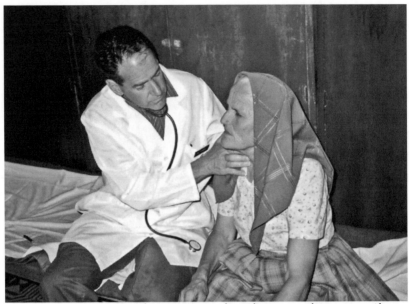

An elderly Romanian woman in distress with a Cardiac Arrhythmia going into heart failure.

They had a lot of skin infections, including bacterial cellulites, fungus infection, and traumatic wounds. We treated the children for bronchitis, pharyngitis and many systemic infections. The adults had arthritis, gastritis and all the other ailments of all the people we usually treat. After seeing all the patients with all their problems, we were invited to sing songs around a campfire. We had a wonderful time of fellowship, singing and laughing and dancing together. There was nothing frightening about these people. They were a delight and a blessing to all of us. We will never forget the Gypsies of Cluj, Romania, and perhaps they won't forget us. All our lives were forever changed by this experience. Man's inhumanity to man was altered this one afternoon to man's care for his fellow man. We were exhausted and went back to our hotel, smelling like sour milk and garbage, but we had an inner glow and satisfaction that was similar to the joy that George exhibited every morning in the clinic. God was teaching us about His love and provision and allowing us to be part of the process. We prepared our medicines that evening for our next clinic in the morning in the rural countryside of Romania.

We went south of the city of Cluj, Romania to a farm community, carrying our medical equipment and medicines to a schoolhouse. Immediately upon arrival, a thin, wiry, woman ran up to me and grabbed my hand and placed it over the left side of her chest against her heart. She didn't speak English and I don't speak Romanian, but I immediately knew what was wrong with her. I didn't have a portable electrocardiogram machine with me. I have been a medical doctor for over thirty-five years and I have had a lot of experience in diagnostic physical medicine without the availability of high tech equipment. I had her lie down on a school desk and I listened to her heart. Her heart rate was one hundred and eighty and she was becoming symptomatic. This meant, she was short of breath and going into congestive heart failure. She seemed to indicate she was having chest pain. She didn't have peripheral edema, (fluid in her ankles) or pulmonary edema (fluid in her chest) and was not as yet in heart failure, but these disasters were impending. If she had presented herself to an emergency room in the states, I would have ordered lab tests, an electrocardiogram, and placed her on a heart monitor. She would have been administered intravenous anti-arrhythmic medicines, and possibly called a cardiologist for a consultation. Obviously, none of this was available to me. I had to act immediately, without hesitation, as this short of breath woman, clutching her chest would have gone into congestive heart failure or had a heart attack in front of me and possibly would have died.

I made a quick assumption that she had atrial tachycardia, and I had her hold her breath and pushed on her carotid artery for five seconds. Nothing happened. We repeated the maneuver, but this time I showed her how to bear down while holding her breath and again I pushed on her carotid artery. During this procedure, (the valsalva maneuver), I was monitoring her pulse. Her heart paused for what seemed to be an unbearably along time. Her heart began to beat again at a regular eighty beats per minute. She smiled, jumped up off the desk and began kissing me. We gave her an oral beta-blocker to try to prevent a recurrence of this episode and gave her lanoxin with the instructions to take it for a few days if her heart began to race again. The pastor of the church assured us, he would get her to a local doctor in the future. I doubt this would happen but we had "saved" this woman's life.

She probably had paroxysmal atrial tachycardia, broken by this Valsalva maneuver. It all happened in a few short minutes. We all settled down to a less eventful medical clinic. Would that woman have died, if we were not there? I don't know. But for me, it was worth the trip. I

A relieved woman after her ordeal

am a firm believer in the providential control of God, which we rarely acknowledge. When we are late getting on the road, maybe we missed an accident. When our plans don't work out, maybe it was for the best. When we are unable to succeed at our ideas maybe it saved us harm in the future. I don't believe God manages us like puppets but I believe God protects and blesses His people with His providential care. Only God sees the big picture and therefore has the foreknowledge to help us in our situations. There is a wonderful example of being in the right place at the right time in the story of Esther in the Bible. Esther, a Jew, was chosen to be the queen in the Medo-Persian Empire because of her beauty. There arose a plot to kill all the Jews, which was discovered by her uncle. He told her to plead for her people to the king, but Esther told him that it would risk her life to approach the king without being summoned. Her uncle Mordecai replies," who can say but that God has brought you into the palace for just such a time as this?" In God's providential care, we may have been brought to Romania for just such a time as this.

This hearty Romanian, peasant woman reminded me of my wiry, strong hard-hitting grandmother Anne. She immigrated to the United States in 1904, from the border of Romania and Russia. She never complained and had thin muscular arms just like this woman. She was kind and caring and was always trying to feed me. She had a heart of gold but she was tough as nails. From my perspective, she was a very religious orthodox Jewish woman, who tried to keep the Jewish dietary laws including a strictly kosher home and observed all the High Holy days, (Jewish festivals). I remember spending the Passover holidays with her and my grandfather in Brooklyn, New York, being fed kreplach and matzabri (please forgive my phonetic spelling) without any bread to be found in the entire house. I recall going to the fish market, picking out a live fish from the tank for dinner or going to the poultry market selecting a live chicken and waiting for the butcher to kill it, followed by my grandmother plucking it's feathers. In this butcher shop, there were feathers everywhere and all over us. These outings with my grandmother were more exciting then playing with any type of toy. She was not very physical in displaying her love for me, but I knew she loved me. She got the message across. I learned from my grandmother that loving a child is not enough. They must understand and know that you love them. They must get the message without a double meaning and without any doubts. They must be able to rely on the knowledge of your love to create a stable platform to build their own personalities and their own life. When my children were young, I would ask them how they knew that I loved them. Their answers were very revealing. They said that they knew I loved them because I spent time with them. They understood my love by my advice and admonishments. They observed my love by my interaction with my wife, their mother. They experienced my love by my words of encouragement and even my yelling at them and punishing them. They knew that I loved them because of my hugging and holding and kissing and general concern for them. I have always expressed my love for my children and made sure they got the message. Silent loving is not enough. Love must be expressed and understood to be effective. My Grandma Anne demonstrated her love for me by spending time with me, helping me and feeding me. Love can take many forms, but it must be received and acknowledged. She also expressed her love through her religion. I realized it was my grandma and not my grandfather, who upheld the religious traditions of our family. They were called orthodox Jews because they observed the orthodox cultural laws but I later came to realize that their religion was traditional and cultural without a true relationship to the Creator God of the Bible. I say this because many of my Jewish relatives, including my mother and sister doubt the existence of God. My sister observes the Jewish holidays and goes to a temple "religiously". She had tried Cabalism, Buddhism, and is now into Zen Buddhism. I asked her, how she got into Zen Buddhism and she said, "My rabbi turned me onto it." Can you imagine a trained rabbi, a teacher of Judaism, who went to rabbinical seminary believing in Zen Buddhism? Where is the relationship with the God of Abraham, Isaac, and Jacob? My mother will tell you that of course she believes in God, but she believes everything is God: the trees, the earth, the sky and all the people. She doesn't know it, but she is a pantheist. It may amaze the reader that a large proportion of American Jews are atheistic but still staunch Jews in their "Jewishness." I had a medical colleague, who was proud to tell me that his son was accepted to rabbinical seminary. He told me that it was harder to get into seminary then medical school, both academically and psychologically. I asked him a question that I probably should not have asked, as it destroyed his joy. I asked him, "Does your son believe in God?" He looked at me, turned to walk away as he murmured, "He hasn't decided yet." Where is his relationship to God and how does the seminary judge their applicant's qualifications? My grandmother was a culturally religious Jew, but at the time, I didn't understand that religious Jews might not believe in a real Creator God of the Bible.

My grandmother had one strange habit we never knew about until her death. She was a closet smoker but she wouldn't smoke on the Sabbath. Saturday night after the Sabbath, she would smoke a cigarette in the bathroom at the top of the stairs. The night of her death, she smoked her cigarette, blew the smoke out the bathroom window and

Americans and Romanian gypsies singing in the city dump.

proceeded to walk down the steps. Since she hadn't smoked for the past twenty-four hours, she got light-headed and fell down the stairs. She lay at the base of the stairs and when we all arrived to help, she said in Yiddish, "leave me alone" and she died. I always remembered that she was a self contained amazingly strong and independent woman in life and even in death. After her death, my grandfather, never attended the synagogue again. She was the "religious" one and not my grandfather.

The Romanian woman in this village was somebody's grandmother and she looked just like my Grandma Anne. She was of the same hearty stock as my grandma. These Romanian people, under communism were not allowed to worship God openly until after the fall of the Soviet block of nations. They are now flocking to the churches but

Gavi Moldavan, a pastor and church planter proudly display the American and Romanian Flags in his office

have reached out to new churches less representative of the communist regime affiliated with the Romanian Orthodox Church. Our hosts in Romania were church planters who had exciting testimonies of how God was working in these small Romanian villages.

One of these church planter pastors went to a remote village to start a Bible-based Christ-centered church. He made a visit to the local Orthodox priest, to the local chief of police and to the mayor of the town to tell them of his plan to hold an outdoor service on the next Saturday in the town square, so as not to compete with the normal Romanian Orthodox service on Sunday. The priest was very angry about the perceived "competition" but was told by the mayor and the chief of police that this young pastor had the right to conduct a service in the town square. The young pastor placed flyers around the village and surrounding areas and that Saturday about thirty people attended the service. He prayed and just as he began his sermon, the priest started to ring the loud church bells that effectively drowned out his message. No one could hear him and he was about to disband the group, when hundreds of village people descended on the town square. It seemed that ringing the church bells on a non-church day was a signal to the people to come to the town square. They saw the pastor and his group and they all joined the service and due to the hundreds of town's people, the priest didn't dare to ring the bells again. The bells had drawn the people to hear the word of God. God certainly uses human circumstances, even negative situations to advance His kingdom.

Another pastor told us his miraculous story. He decided to bring a brass band to another village for a Christian music concert. All the arrangements were made but the weather forecast for that day was rain. He was told not to go to the town but he decided to trust God. They set up all their instruments in the town square and started to tune up while twenty to thirty people gathered in the square. There was a cloud burst and it started to pour which made it difficult to play and the people were getting wet. The pastor realized that he had made a mistake but wondered to himself why God had not honored their commitment. As they began to pack up their instruments, hundreds of farmers from the surrounding countryside arrived from all directions to hear the music in the rain. It seemed that there had been a draught for months and the prayers of the local Orthodox Romanian Church had not produced rain. The villagers felt that the Christian music was directly singing to the Lord and that He had blessed the village with rain. They joined the group with singing and dancing to the Lord in praise of His provision of rain. After the music, the young pastor gave a stirring sermon to several hundred of the town's people about the loving kindness of God and His concern for His people. Man may gather a few people to hear the word of God but God gathers hundreds and thousands to bless all.

After one of our medical clinics in a small farm community with many hardy elderly people, we shared farm fresh baked goods and singing with these robust farmers. I sat between two strong middle-aged women and I was back in the comfort and contentment of my Grandma Anne. I sat there thinking of my grandmother and the time and love we shared together. I thought about the fact that God loves all people but He allows for their free will and it is up to them to voluntarily accept His free-will offer of His Son. My own grandmother didn't know the Son and I wish she had known Him, as I miss her and want to see her again. Most Christians and even non-believers have heard the Bible verse of John 3:16. "For God so loved the world that he gave His only begotten Son, that whoever believes in Him shall not perish but have eternal life." The designation of whoever is you and me, but we must believe and this belief is voluntary. If, as a doctor, I diagnose a disease and I prescribe the appropriate medicine but the patient refuses it, then the cure is not available to that patient. It is as if the research to discover that drug was never accomplished for that individual patient. Individuals must avail themselves of the cure. The one who denies Jesus is still under God's condemnation for their sins, as if Jesus never came for them. They refuse the cure and eternal life with God. It is a very personal decision. God desires that all men should come to Him and live eternally in heaven. The entire Bible is about getting man back to a right relationship to God after the fall of man in the Garden of Eden. The Bible spends only five words on the creation of the cosmos: it says, "He made the stars also." However, the rest of the Bible, written by forty different authors over two thousand years covering many human topics is concerned with man's return to this right relationship with God. God is interested in us. We are His most grand design and He loves us more than any of His other creations. He loves all peoples, even those that reject Him. Jesus wept over those who refused to believe in Him. After my grandmother's death, it seemed as if I lost touch with my grandfather and we didn't celebrate the Jewish festivals together or really relate to each other in any way. It was my grandmother who was the cultural Jew and kept the extended family together, and not my grandfather.

My grandfather did not have a relationship with God but he sure had a relationship with capitalism and the automobile. He worked very hard as a window cleaner and in those days, especially the depression period, money was tight, but my grandfather would buy a new Oldsmobile every two years. My grandmother would pinch pennies but my grandfather would buy that brand new expensive automobile in spite of their economic status. He was a capitalist and made Henry Ford and his friend Harvey Firestone multi-millionaires. It was an economy based on timed obsolescence and it worked. My grandfather was only interested in himself and his beautiful new Oldsmobile.

When my daughter Faith and I were in Romania, the people looked a lot like my family, and it brought back the memories and stories my mother relayed to me about my family's beginnings in the United States. My immigrant grandfather came from somewhere on the border of the Ukraine, Poland, Hungary and Romania. These borders had changed based on many past European wars. He arrived in the foreign land of America, speaking a foreign language, not knowing the customs, and never having lived in a big city like New York. Most immigrants came to the United States to seek freedom and opportunity. My grandfather had to come to the United States because he killed a man in his village and he needed to escape from the authorities, and the town's people wanted to string him up!

He was a stocky bullish man about five feet ten inches tall but looking much bigger then his height. He had a fierce competitive attitude, and a singleness of purpose; caring only for himself. This Jewish man was the town bully in a Gentile village. He was hated by these people and tolerated by his landsman (Jewish neighbors). His family farmed in this border village in the Russian sphere of influence. He was uncontrollable and his boldness was all the more remarkable considering that he was a minority in a non-Jewish village. He was the black sheep of the family. The Pogroms were already in progress and this Jewish man was the town bully in a Protestant hamlet. In fact, I was told that townspeople stepped off the wooden sidewalk when, Jake Frankel, passed by. In those days, stepping off the curb was no small thing. You stepped off the sidewalk and into knee-deep mud and manure. His own people tolerated him because they needed him as an enforcer and because he was "family." This "bulvon," headstrong male was the patriarch of my family in the United States. My heritage doesn't contain pilgrims, or

My daughter, Faith, giving out small toys to the gypsy children in front of their "homes" in the city dump.

Jamestown survivors or freedom-loving adventurers, but a murderer who escaped justice.

Jake's younger brother had been in a fight with a boy his own age and came home as the loser: torn and tattered. My grandfather, who used his brawn before his brain, went to this boy's house and beat up the boy's father. He dragged this man out of his house in front of a crowd, pounding him into submission. He was proud of himself until the man didn't move. He had been beaten to death. Now the town had a reason to hang my grandfather. He ran to his home and was hidden by his relatives in the barn. He was kept on the run by the police, until his family was able to smuggle him out of the country. It became too risky to hide him. The villagers took up a collection and he was able to get a boat after traveling across Poland to the Baltic Sea, then to the North Sea and then through the Atlantic, to America. This was the austere beginning of my family in the new world. It was less historic than the landing of the Mayflower, but nevertheless, the launching of my family in America, was brought about for reasons of freedom; the freedom from a hangman's noose.

Freedom has always been the hallmark of our society and we have always guarded it and fought for its cause. I remember my anti-Vietnam War position in the sixties, tempered with my intense feelings for freedom for our country and all peoples. I had marched on Washington D.C. in 1969, protesting the war, but in 1972, I found myself in the United States Army being trained in Fort Sam Houston, Texas headed for Vietnam. I was a partially trained surgeon and I knew that I would be sent to a front line M.A.S.H. unit. The fully trained surgeons were stationed in Japan where the wounded were airlifted to large well-equipped hospitals. I had only one year of surgical training and was slated for surgical triage. In spite of my negative feelings about the war, I felt it was not only my duty to go but also my responsibility to my country for all it had done for me. I knew that I was no better than anyone else and if my neighbors had to serve, then it was my task as an American to do the same. I was trained for a frontline M.A.S.H. unit in San Antonio, Texas and ten days before I was scheduled to ship out, I got a very mysterious life changing phone call.

Romanian village peasants in our medical clinic. They all look like my grandparents.

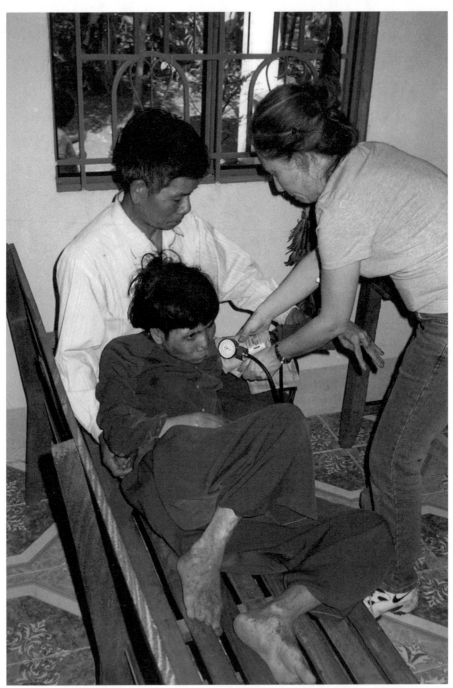

A permanently crippled, blind man brought to our medical clinic for help. We did what we could to alleviate some of his pain and suffering. His only real hope is God and a better home in heaven.

Ambivalence About Vietnam

It was July 1972. I had completed one year of surgical residency at the U.C.L.A.-Wadsworth V.A. and I was offered the chief residency of the five-year surgical program. It was an honor that I had earned by working very hard during the previous year in training. This tribute created a major problem for me concerning my future plans.

When I first applied to the surgical department of the V.A.-U.C.L.A. program, I was interviewed by Dr. Earl Gordon, the chief of the surgical department. He accepted me in his highly competitive, desirable program, but told me that I was only guaranteed the first year of the surgical residency. I was delighted with this offer because that was exactly what I wanted, as I planned to be a family doctor and not a surgeon. In 1972, there wasn't a family practice residency program in this country, and I decided to make up my own. I had taken one year of straight medical internship to be followed by this one year of surgical residency. This was acceptable to all the parties.

As a surgical first year resident, we were allowed to perform the "minor" cases. While I was a medical intern treating various medical diseases, I naturally had to take a detailed history from every patient, accompanied by a complete physical examination. These patients had various surgical problems as well as medical emergencies. We treated them for their medical problems and I recorded their names on a notepad to call them at a later date to complete their elective surgical procedures. These procedures were hernias, cholecystectomies (gall bladder extraction), and various "lumps and bumps." I became the busiest first year surgical resident and acquired the most surgical experience. As a result of my surgical schedule and developed expertise, the chief of surgery had recommended me for the full five-year program. I was congratulated for receiving this wonderful opportunity and honor. I was slated to be the chief resident in the future. I never had the desire to become a surgeon and it wasn't in my plans, but it was now in their plans for my life. As I've said before, freedom and opportunity are very important to me and reflect my American patriotism and love for this country. I was also very headstrong, stubborn, and prideful.

I made an appointment to talk to Dr. Gordon, and upon greeting me with a big smile that I had never seen before, he vigorously shook my hand and welcomed me to the surgical fraternity. I relayed my plans to him and he was very silent and obviously stunned and insulted. I had re-

Fishing in a rice paddy in Vietnam

jected his program. After an unbearable silence, he detailed how I was the one with a major problem and not him or the program. It was 1972 and the Vietnam War was still being waged. The chief of staff of this important, prestigious surgical program informed me, "Son, You can be one of my surgical residents, or be on the front lines." No one was going to scare me or make me do what I didn't want to do. I could have received more training and waited out the war as many others had done in the medical profession. No one was going to run my life. Two weeks later I received a different congratulatory letter, and one month later, I was driving to Fort Sam Houston, Texas, to be trained to go to Vietnam. Stubbornness and pride had gotten my family into trouble before, in the form of my murderous grandfather, our patriarch. I suppose, I have some of his traits.

When my grandfather came to this country, after hiding from the authorities in his native land, you might have thought he had learned his lesson and taken a low profile. However, he continued to harass the people of New York in his same bullying style. I personally witnessed my grandfather at the age of sixty-seven, beat up a man for going through a red light, because the man made him stop short. To this day, I believe it was really my grandfather's fault. He couldn't read English and had trouble observing the traffic laws.

So when, Jacob Frankel, arrived in New York City via Ellis Island with the millions of other hardy, hungry, freedom yearning people, he carved out a tough life for himself in the land of plenty. Jake, young and headstrong, pounded the streets to obtain work and achieve his rightful place in the American society. By ingenuity, he developed a window-cleaning route, but he came to an impasse. The Mafia, or at least a group of Italians who pawned themselves off as the Mafioso, made a visit to my grandfather. It turned out that you had to have a "contract" to clean a storefront window in New York. In fact, the Mafia, like the unions after them, would not let you clean your own windows. My grandfather didn't know that the window-cleaning business was the sole property of these few hard working Italian immigrants. He surveyed new stores and signed up his new clients. He was immediately

A Vietnamese orphanage where "His Healing Hands" did physical examinations on all the children and staff.

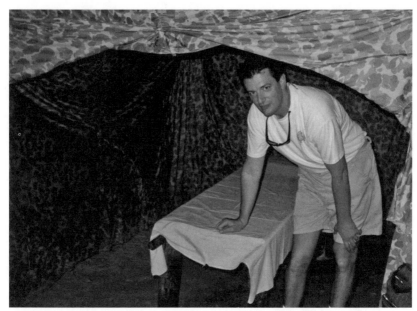

Vietcong living quarters in the Tunnels of Kuchi under
an American base outside of Saigon.

told by his Italian "neighbors" to, "Get off our turf." Jake had always
figured that the world was his turf and nobody pushed him around.
Two Mafia tough guys were sent out to handle this upstart. They returned from their encounter with Jake Frankel, with ballooned up eyes
and cauliflower ears. Their bosses sent out more representatives, but

Pungi sticks, tipped with human feces in a hidden pit, to
cause American casualties.

the results were the same. Jake was beginning to like New York City. It was just his cup of borscht. Believe it or not this group of short friendly Italian Americans accepted my grandfather's competition. Why bother with one man making an honest living? It was the American way. Either, he was too much of a small fry, or the torpedoes were needed for more important work. In any case, let history record, that Jake Frankel, a Polish, Russian immigrant, beat the Mafia in New York City at the turn of the century. It was peaceful coexistence. Jake prospered, as did the millions of other hard-driving immigrants in this new country with unlimited opportunity.

Jennifer Walker getting a ride on a Moped with her new Vietnamese friend.

Politically, I was not in favor of the Vietnam War and had been caught up in the sixties with the anti-war crowd. I was involved with the marches, the music and the "scene." I was a twenty-six year old easterner, brainwashed by the media. I was at a very impressionable age. When I received my congratulatory letter from the Department of the Army, theory had to be replaced by realism. I was against the war but I was an American first and not any more unique than anyone else. If oth-

A Vietnamese house with a view of the city dump

ers had to serve, then why not me? I had spent four years in high school, four years in college, four years in medical school, one year in internship, and one year in surgical residency, and I was on the way to war.

I spent six weeks in training at Fort Sam Houston. They taught us how to shoot an M14, use a compass, and handle being exposed to

Garbage and refuse surround the Vietnamese village

a nerve gas attack. We practiced debriding wounds of a goat that had been shot and taught us a smattering of warfare techniques and drills. I was a captain in the United States Army and was about to ship out for deployment in Vietnam in ten days. I was scared but I had confidence in the men around me and was resigned to serve my country. There was a phone call for me. I am not good at remembering names, but I will never forget the name of Major Lacy, whom I have never met to this day. It seemed that Major Lacy was in Washington, D.C. and had a map of the world behind his desk, with a pin in this map for the location of every doctor in the American army. I was a pin on this map, located in

Our His Healing Hands medical staff and our Vietnamese hosts enjoying a relaxing luncheon outside of Vung Tau.

San Antonio, Texas about to be moved to Da Nang, Vietnam. He asked me if I was willing to go to an induction center, instead of Vietnam. This would be a very boring assignment for a doctor. I agreed and he moved my pin in the map to a new location. That's all it took. It seems as if fate or God had invaded my life and changed my circumstances. I was relieved and grateful but I felt ambivalent and guilty. For thirty years, I've experienced these guilt feelings especially when I later treated injured Vietnam vets in my medical practice. I recently went to Vietnam on a medical missionary trip, in the capacity of a missionary doctor

A Chinese Vietcong soldier now living in the jungle befriends Mark Walker, His Healing Hands division head of South East Asia

treating the poor of Vietnam. My understanding of the "American War" as they call it and my thoughts about the Vietnam War as we call it, have changed. I finally got to Vietnam in the capacity of a doctor but under far different circumstances. At last, I was going to deal with my feelings of guilt and ambivalence.

"His Healing Hands," a short-term medical missionary organization in association with Campus Crusade for Christ flew into Ho Chi Min City, still called Saigon by the inhabitants. We met our pastor host and drove through the countryside to Vung Tau, south of the Mekong Delta. Again, I was ambivalent because I didn't know if the Vietnamese people would accept us, and what my feelings would be. The countryside of Vietnam was absolutely beautiful. The people took us into their homes and were extremely grateful for our medical care. We met with the Vietnam communists and after "formal" negotiations in their office, they allowed us to treat their people. We had to donate money to help build a clinic in Vung Tau. At the time, we believed it to be a camouflaged bribe but we were wrong. Six months later, they invited us to the opening of their clinic with our "His Healing Hands" logo over the clinic door.

We spent a lot of time with the villagers and mountain people. They spoke of the "American War" in different terms than I had ever heard. In the sixties and seventies, the American administration had warned that if we pulled out of Vietnam, there would be a "blood bath." They also said, that the war was not really a civil war but an invasion of Chinese mercenary soldiers occupying Vietnam. I never bought this excuse to go to war. These people, who lived through this period in their country, relayed the true story as they had experienced it. They confirmed the massive invasion of foreign Chinese troops and their brutality to the South Vietnamese. They stated in a shocking disclosure that four million Vietnamese were tortured and murdered after the Americans left South Vietnam, truly a "blood bath." We were told that the South Vietnamese people had always wanted the American presence. They told us about the cruelty of the Vietcong (Chinese Soldiers) and the tunnels of Kuchi and the violence toward the captured American soldiers. We were taken through these tunnels and the torture weapons were on display. I believe that these kind, caring, Christian villagers, who had experienced the war first hand were telling us the truth.

I had watched the body bags of U.S. marines returning home and the myriads of Vietnamese dying on the nightly news. Sometimes, we believe the negative stories of Americans as seen through the eyes of

Alan Martin, giving his Christian testimony between reels of the showing of "The Jesus Film" in the Vietnamese language.

our enemies. We are an extremely giving and compassionate people. There is peace in Vietnam now, but at what cost? The Romans had a term for it. It was the Pax Romana. They "caused" peace in a town by killing all the inhabitants and then declaring the peace. There is now peace in the communist state of Vietnam. It all came true. We should never underestimate the freedom loving American people or the desire for all people's love of freedom. I truly believe that freedom is all people's unalienable right to life, liberty, and the pursuit of happiness and not just our American dream. None of the Americans in Vietnam died in vain.

I am no longer ambivalent about my role or lack of role during the Vietnamese War, and I have even more respect and admiration for our government and the American Armed Forces. We are the most powerful country in the world and we are benevolent and humanitarian. The Vietnamese people were extremely grateful for our medical care and spiritual help. They chauffeured us all around Vung Tau Province. They smiled; they bowed, and were joyous to share the time with us. These people demonstrated forgiveness and brotherhood to our team in the remote rice paddies of Vietnam. Only God can teach this kind of love and forgiveness. The Lord works in mysterious ways and controls both our steps and our stops. He stopped me, as a non-believer from going to Vietnam at the wrong time and paved my steps in going as a believer to share His love through medical missions. His love all over the world to all peoples creates faith and removes all doubt and ambivalence. God always holds up His side of a covenant (deal). My faith was indeed increasing, but I came to realize other aspects of expanding faith. I came to understand that God will increase my faith but I had to handle my side of the agreement with prayer. I came to realize the absolute necessity of prayer, when I should have died on the road from Hyderabad to Vijayawada, India. I don't want to sound off the wall, but maybe I did die on that road.

UH-1 (Huey) helicopter used during the Vietnamese War
(Called the American War in Vietnam) on display in
Saigon (Ho Chi Minh City)

Sherpas carrying produce to the hillside town of Shimla, India.

We Died On An Indian Highway

After crisscrossing the sub-continent of India, from Chenai to Bangalore, to Goa, to Bombay, to Hyderabad, to Vijayawada, to Delhi, to Shimla, to Calcutta and back to Chenai, we didn't see one McDonald restaurant. But what the Indians lacked in hamburgers, they made up with gods. They certainly could put up signs that say, "Over One Billion Served." India seems to have ignored the first and foremost commandment; "Thou shalt have no other gods before me." They have four major religions in India. In Hinduism, Jainism, Buddhism and Sikhism they have literally thousands of gods. They are a very "spiritual" people. Eighty-five per cent of India's one billion plus people are Hindus. They have the third largest Moslem population in the world. Christianity is well down on the list. Whenever our group, "His Healing Hands," returns from a medical missionary trip, everyone at home asks us, "How did it go?" We had a blessed time, treating hundreds of patients, and encouraging thousands of others, however India saddened me. I felt like the apostle Paul looking over the hills of Rome and seeing all the lost people. I remember what Jesus said about His sadness while looking down from the hills of Judea. He would have gathered the people to Himself like a mother hen with her chicks, if they had accepted Him. They didn't recognize Him. These spiritual Indian people were worshiping animals, statues, and mythological gods, and not recognizing the true God. They wanted to fill the void in their hearts, but their emptiness was obvious.

These poor people give their rupees to monkey dolls, dressed in robes, sitting in window boxes. These rupees are collected by white bearded, brightly colored robed, incense burning gurus with very contented smiles. Even the children on their way to school, stop to place a rupee in these drive-thru prayer parlors and place a third eye on their forehead for enlightenment. Their goal is self-awareness and inner tranquility in self-servitude, but it leaves them even more impoverished and barren. These people readily accept Jesus as just another god who has become a freethinking guru.

A typical crowded Indian street with cars, trucks, mopeds, motorcycles, pedestrians, and roaming cattle.

In this impossible atmosphere, God is working through His people. God seems to love to wait until human endeavors fail and then He raises up godly believers to serve Him and present the gospel to a suspicious nation.

Our medical team of "His Healing Hands" staff met wonderful Indian believers dedicating their lives to presenting the gospel of Jesus Christ to the one billion lost of India. We came alongside these gracious believers, lifted them up in the eyes of their own people, medically treated their people, and assured them that Americans cared about them and prayed for them. We are one people, under one Spirit, and under one creator God in the name of Jesus. We were all encouraged and God increased our faith.

On the plane over to India, we met "a want-to-be Sikh." She was dressed in full turban and robes. She appeared very prideful and told us that she was a healer, but just in case "I brought along some antibiotics," as a back-up plan. We went to India without a back-up plan. We only had our belief in a creator God who took human form to die for the forgiveness of our sins and was then resurrected as the first fruits. All we have to do is believe and follow Him. We met this same Sikh on the way back and she was very sick and very disappointed. She had gone to India to become enlightened and bathe in the "holy" waters, but all she received from this "holy" filthy polluted river was severe diarrhea. God protected us, cared for us and allowed us to participate in the process of presenting His love to the people of India. That protection was in fact miraculous. I truly believe we were in a life-threatening situation and we escaped unscathed.

When I returned home from this Indian medical missionary trip, my friend Bob told me that one of the Saturdays while I was gone, he awoke at 1A.M. He said, "I bolted up and felt the need to pray for you." I thanked him for praying, but didn't think about it any further. The next day was Thanksgiving and my brother-in-law told me that on Saturday, while I was in India, he awoke at 2A.M, startled with an impelling desire to pray for me. I likewise thanked him for praying. The next day, I went to my office to look at my itinerary. India is 13 ½ hours ahead of the west coast of the United States. I calculated that on Sunday at 11A.M., we were on the road from Vijayawada, to Hyderabad; at the very time my friend Bob and my brother-in-law were awakened to pray for our group. Suddenly, I realized we should have died on that road or maybe as strange as it may seem, we did die.

We had just finished our medical clinics in Vijayawada, and we needed to drive to Hyderabad to board a plane to Delhi. We told our

A busy street in Vijayawada, India

Oxen on the road from Vijayawada to Hyderabad, India

driver that we needed to be on time for that plane and we were six hours away. He said that he could drive the road in five hours. What a mistake we made to rush this driver. He drove like a man bent on destruction. We were on a two-lane road without shoulders alongside buses, trucks, oxen, goats, sheep, tractors, pedestrians, motorcycles, and rickshaws in addition to free roaming cows. Every few minutes, the driver would pass a slow moving vehicle by pulling out into oncoming traffic. I was seated directly behind the driver and I noticed his lack of any mirrors whatsoever. In place of the side mirrors were the remnants of mirror stems where they had been knocked off in sideswiping other buses and trucks. Several times, it appeared as if we scraped the paint off our taxi, while passing oncoming trucks at 80-90 kms/hr. I could see our "passing" better than anyone.

He pulled out to pass, hoping that the truck in front of us would slow down. Approaching us rapidly was another truck passing an on-coming bus, but our driver was committed or should have been. He tried to slip around the truck that we were overtaking, approaching an intersection. An ox was partially standing in our lane. We had no place to go and I "knew," we were dead. I could foresee a head-on collision, spinning and rolling with trucks, buses, cars, and animals on the road. I remember thinking that in the past, I had wondered about my reaction just before I knew I would die. My colleagues in the taxi later said I had a strange look on my face at that moment. I must have blinked, because a split second later, we were beyond this intersection.

Although this is a weird statement, I truly believe we were to die on that road. I believe the prayers of my support team in the United States, at exactly the specific time of this incident, affected God's provision for us and spared our lives. I teach a Bible study, and on the next Sunday, I related this extraordinary, weird and wonderful story to my class. The members of my class had also been praying for this Indian medical missionary project. Three of the attendees of the class stood up and said that they likewise awoke at about 1a.m. that same night and felt an urgent need to pray for us. It appears that God affects even our sleep and our dreams and awakens us to pray for others. In changing the course of events, He provides for His people and allows us to be part of that process. The Bible says our prayers will be answered if we pray in the will of God. I want to be living and praying in the will of God, so my prayers will be answered. Therefore I must redirect my desires and needs and wishes to God's desires for His kingdom and my life.

Since that medical trip, I make sure that I have prayer warriors back home as our support team. I won't leave home without it. Prayer is not magic, but I know from first-hand experience that it not only works but it is imperative for all of us. God loves to answer our prayers and we can never ask too much. He will grant our prayers as long as it is His will. God has increased my faith but prayer is an inherent part of that process. God allows us to be part of the process for our own benefit. When we pray, we hear our own requests, acknowledge our need for God and have a direct relationship with Him. There are many very elegant religions in the world. Man has a basic need to fill a void in his heart that is purely spiritual. Christianity is not a religion but a relationship with God, the Father, through Jesus, the Son. This is a strange statement especially coming from an orthodox Jew who believes in the God of Abraham, Isaac, and Jacob.

When I tell others that I believe Jesus is the messiah that the Jews have been waiting for all these years, they say "Oh you have converted." However, I consider myself more Jewish than ever. In fact, in order to remain Jewish, I had to accept Jesus as my messiah. Bear with me and I will explain that statement. As already stated, I was brought up in an orthodox Jewish environment. I attended an orthodox Hebrew school, participated in Jewish ethnic clubs, and went to the synagogue every Saturday. I was very involved with reading the Jewish Bible (the Old Testament), and all of the Jewish cultural activities. At the age of thirteen, I was bar-mitzvahed, and continued in Hebrew school. I was offered to attend a Hebrew high school but I wanted to play high school basketball, so I elected to go to public high school. I stopped going to the synagogue except for the High Holy Days of Rosh Hashanah. and Yom Kippur. I continued to faithfully read the Jewish scriptures, study the prophesies of the coming messiah, and ask God to reveal Himself to me as the scriptures advise. The Hebrew Scriptures state that if you ask God to reveal Himself to you and you keep an open mind, He will give you enough "light" to start to understand your relationship to Him. Depending on what you do with that "light," God will give you more understanding based on your ability to absorb that knowledge.

Since childhood, I have always thought of death, due to my father's illness and his eventual death when I was eight years old. I wanted to comprehend: who I was, where I had come from, where I was going, and where I would eventually end up. The Old Testament provided me with some of the answers and the biblical poetry gave me sound advice on how to live. It didn't satisfy my desire to understand life; it's meaning and eternity.

My New York Italian friends believed in Jesus as the messiah. We Jews believe the messiah is yet to come and we are awaiting and praying for His arrival. In fact, my relatives, neighbors, and religious teachers made fun of the misguided Gentiles and their television healing Sunday morning shows. I loved to watch Oral Roberts heal these sick people on Sunday morning. The invalids would be brought to him on stage. He would pray for them, lay hands on them and they would be healed and walk off the stage without help. If only this could happen to my wheelchair-bound father. As a non-believer I doubted these miraculous healings but they intrigued me. I understood about an all-powerful God who could do miracles but my faith needed to grow. Nevertheless, these programs fascinated me. I remember during the yearly Passover service, we would pour a cup of wine for Elijah. We knew that the prophets said that Elijah had to come before the messiah. We poured the cup of redemption for Elijah. We opened the door but he never came and it was always said, "maybe next year." In hindsight, I now think that it was the Holy Spirit giving me some "light" and a desire for more knowledge. I literally wrestled with the Holy Spirit. I didn't feel a need for any part of Christianity; after all I am a Jew. I already had a beautiful religion in Judaism. Now I understand that I had a religion but not a relationship with God.

As I grew older, I continued to read the Old Testament, but the answers and the complete story was just not there for me. Many individuals will relate that coming to a knowledge of Jesus Christ was out of personal suffering. This was not the case with me. After graduating high school, college, medical school, internship, residency and two years in the army, I opened a private family medical practice. I was married, had children and had a blessed life, without complaints. However, again, the answers were not there. Life was great but as Peggy Lee's sad song asks, "Is that all there is?" was a question that I asked myself frequently. I knew that there had to be more to life then pleasing oneself, helping others and leaving a "mark" on the world. I have always had a desire to aid others but even humanitarian work didn't satisfy me. Something was missing. It was a personal relationship with the Creator God of the universe. I lived on a ranch in California with my wife and three children. My life was blessed with good health, a good wife, great kids, a wonderful profession, beautiful surroundings and economic stability. God works in mysterious ways, maybe in the form of a visiting brother-in-law.

My brother-in-law, graduated college and "visited" us for two weeks, but wound up staying in our guest room for two years. If you have a guest room, I advise you to paint the walls purple with stripes or polka dots, as a hint to all your future visitors. Actually, George was a wonderful guest, and we had very intellectually stimulating conversations. He knew that I was Jewish and that I had studied the Jewish Bible. He was a born-again Christian who had originally been brought up in the Greek Orthodox religion. He loved the entire Bible, both the Old Testament and the New Testament. He asked me, "What do you think of the New Testament?" I told him that it was an anti-Semitic book and that it was junk. I had just insulted the basis of his entire belief system, but he didn't get angry. He asked me, "What part of the book didn't you like?" I said, "I don't know, because I never read it." I had just given an opinion about something that I knew nothing about. This was the epitome of foolishness for a so-called educated man. After my thoughtless comment, I decided to read the Christian Bible.

I started with the book of Matthew, expecting to discover a hateful, mythical manuscript, of anti-Jewish propaganda, based on a world of anti-Semitism. The history of the Jews is a history of trials, tribulations, and tests from a hate filled prejudiced anti-Semitic world. The Jews had suffered at the hands of the Babylonians, the Assyrians, anti-Semitism of Europe with the Programs, the Spanish inquisition, and the Islamic invasion up to and including the Moors of Spain. This history culminated in the attempt of Hitler in the "final solution" to finally wipe out all the remaining Jews. But God is faithful and is a covenant keeping God. In 1949, He resurrected the nation of Israel and during my reading of the Book of Matthew; He performed a work in my heart. I discovered a very "Jewish" book written in the same style as my Bible; the Old Testament. I had studied the Five Books of Moses and the Prophets, and the Poetry. I believed in the God of Abraham, Isaac, and Jacob. I believed that the Bible was the word of God, and since the fall of Adam and Eve, we have been waiting for a Messiah to lead our people, who was a prophet like Moses. The prophets talked about this Messiah, but I didn't understand about the Suffering Servant or the Conquering King. Likewise, the Psalms talked about the salvation of the Jews through the God of Israel. There were a lot of disconnected facts in my brain but I couldn't connect the dots until I read this book written by a Jewish tax collector who was working for the Romans against the Jews.

When I graduated college, I had to decide whether to follow my love of history and become a history professor or go into the medical profession. I chose both. I went to medical school and continued to study history. This book of Matthew was consistent with the history books and first century accounts of Roman and Middle Eastern history. It discussed prophecy based on Old Testament predictions. I continued to read, and was amazed at the references to fulfilled prophecy. It started with the genealogy of Jesus, indicating his ties to the line of David, going back to Abraham. This fulfilled Old Testament prophecy. It stated that He was born in Bethlehem in Judea, another fulfilled prophecy of the coming Messiah. The Jewish prophet Isaiah specifically and in great detail described how the Messiah would suffer and die by crucifixion, which at the time had not been devised as a method of death. The entire Old Testament repeatedly stated that only God would save His people and He was the only source of our salvation and yet it also stated that the Messiah was our salvation. It was logical that God was the only

Cows wandering on the streets of New Deli.

possible qualified Messiah. Matthew stated that a man named John who was a prophet, was a forerunner to make the way straight for the Messiah. He was asking the people to repent in order to prepare themselves for the Messiah. This corresponded to the prophecy of Elijah, who was to return to get the people ready for the Messiah.

Jesus performed miraculous deeds in front of eyewitnesses and explained the law as no one had ever done. I was amazed at the insight, relevance, and common sense of his explanation of my book, the Old Testament. No one had ever said, "love your enemies," instead of, "an eye for an eye" in order to stop feuds, or consider both men and women "equal before God," or "turn the other cheek." He spoke in parables that demonstrated more wisdom than any books or philosophers that I have ever read. He broke down prejudices between Jews and Gentiles, men and women, priests and lay people, and between the rich and poor. He spoke of the future and the eternal kingdom of God, and He declared who He was. He claimed to be equal to God, the Father. He claimed to be the giver of life. He claimed that He could raise the dead and He did it, again in front of eyewitnesses. He claimed to be the final judge and to determine each man's destiny. Finally, He claimed to always do the will of the Father. He claimed to be God. Who was this man called Jesus? I had to decide for myself. Was he just a prophet as many other religions claim today? Was he just a great teacher or was he another religious

An Indian bazaar in Vigiaywada, India.

fanatic? He could be any of these if he wasn't God but he claimed to be God and if he wasn't God and the Messiah, then he was a liar and not a good person at all. Again, Who is this Jesus of Nazareth?

I have already stated that as a Jew, I believed in the God of Abraham, Isaac and Jacob. It is interesting to note that my father's name was Abraham. My grandfather's name was Jacob and my father's brother's name was Isaac. I believed in the scriptures and I was waiting for the Messiah with all the rest of the Jewish nation. I had to think with an open mind, in a reasonable logical fashion, without emotion or pure feelings. Who was this Jesus? I came to a startling conclusion. If He was the God of Abraham, Isaac, and Jacob, then in order to remain Jewish, I had to accept Him as the Messiah and my Lord and Savior. I realized that the most Jewish thing that I could ever do was to accept the Jewish Messiah. This was not an easy decision for an orthodox Jew. I love being a Jew and I love the state of Israel. There has never been a country in the history of the world that was so utterly devastated as Israel and literally resurrected from it's own ashes. It was God's promise, and I also claimed the promise that if I sought God with an open mind, He would reveal Himself to me. I asked myself "What would the Messiah have to do, and what prophecies would He have to fulfill to claim Messiah ship?" I realized that Jesus had already fulfilled all those prophecies. He had performed miracles in front of eyewitnesses, including making the blind see, the lame walk, raise the dead and appear to over five hundred eyewitnesses after His own resurrection. He was born in the line of David and everything that He did was consistent with the Old Testament. He had predicted His own future and even controlled natural phenomenon. I couldn't deny it. Believe me, I tried. I knew that if I accepted Jesus as the Messiah, as God, that my family would think either I had a brain tumor or that I was insane and possibly disown me. I had looked for God all my life and it was obvious to me that Jesus was the anointed one. I knew that He must be truly God.

God is faithful. I realized that Jesus was the Messiah as He claimed and I have continued to worship the God of Abraham, Isaac, and Jacob, to this day. His name is Yeshua, the Messiah, the Christ. It took me a long time to even say the name of Jesus, since I had become so prejudiced and indoctrinated with fear of the Christian world. My life changed radically after my decision.

I had always rejected blind faith, but this was historically and biblically accurate. In the past, I assumed that the offer of eternal life was an excuse for Christians to make death more palatable. As a doctor, I had seen many people die and the believers did seem to accept their fate with more joy and acceptance than non-believers. It is now apparent that this joyfulness and equanimity is not an excuse to believe but a result of this belief in an eternal life in the presence of God. Even though I formally believed in God, I only relied on myself; a very lonely position. I had stopped praying or relying on the Bible for comfort or wisdom, and had never depended on wise biblical counsel from other believers. I now can go directly to God in prayer and read His word and get wise guidance from mature believers. It doesn't mean I don't trust myself. I do, but now I have God and His people available to me. I remember when I went to bed at night and shut the light, I felt all alone and it was a very frightening and forlorn sensation. Now this feeling will instantly disappear when I think of God's love and sacrifice for me.

My generation that grew up in the sixties worshipped freedom and independence to "do their own thing." It was a time of free love, freethinking, and freedom from all obligations. The idea of communes and loving everyone with benevolence, generosity, and flower power was the mantra of all college students; sprinkled with drugs, music, and unlimited personal freedom as long as it didn't hurt others. They didn't want a book of rules and regulations to stifle their self-rule. For years I would recite the line from Chris Christopherson's song, "Me and Bobby

An Indian version of a "supermarket."

McGee." "Freedom is just another word for nothing left to lose." We may have considered the Bible as well written literature and even full of interesting historical vignettes but to obey it would mean loss of autonomy and independence. It was all based on a lie that we are in control of our own destiny and that "God was Dead," a headline that actually appeared on the cover of Life magazine at the time. Our so-called freedom did hurt others and ourselves. In the medical profession, we are now diagnosing hepatitis C in fifty-year-old patients who snorted cocaine or used intravenous psychedelic drugs. Aids has been the scourge of humanity all over the planet from unsafe sexual activities. Doing our own thing was self-destructive and destructive to others. It was against our own nature and God. It didn't make us freer. It placed me in self-induced captivity. After accepting Jesus as the true God, I have become freer than I have ever been; free from sin, free from anxiety, and free to be the person that I was created to be. I now realize that freedom is just another word for giving it all to God and trusting in Him alone. I am also more Jewish than ever. The entire Bible now makes sense to me. The story of Abraham, obeying God to sacrifice his only son, Isaac; was a preview of God the Father sacrificing His only begotten Son, Jesus. Abraham had told his servants to wait at the base of Mount Moriah for both him and his son's return. He knew God would raise his son from the dead if he sacrifices Isaac. Abraham was told that he would be a blessing to the "nations." In Hebrew, the word is goyoim, meaning non-Jewish. How was Abraham going to bless the nations? It is now clear that He would do this through the belief in the Jewish Messiah, Jesus. It was now obvious why the rabbis say that Joseph was a type or foreshadowing of the Messiah because he would suffer for his people. And I now understand how Isaiah could talk about a suffering servant and a ruling king. It all makes perfect sense and it is comprehensible to me. But the most exciting part for me is that I know God, and He has a plan for me, and I want to fulfill that plan to His glory.

God has increased my faith and has allowed me to be part of the process through prayer and has made me conscious of His providential care. This means that God is not like Elvis who has left the arena, leaving man to figure out his own destiny. He is active in the world today. I became very aware of this fact on a separate trip when "His Healing Hands" medical missionary organization returned to India to include both medical and dental care.

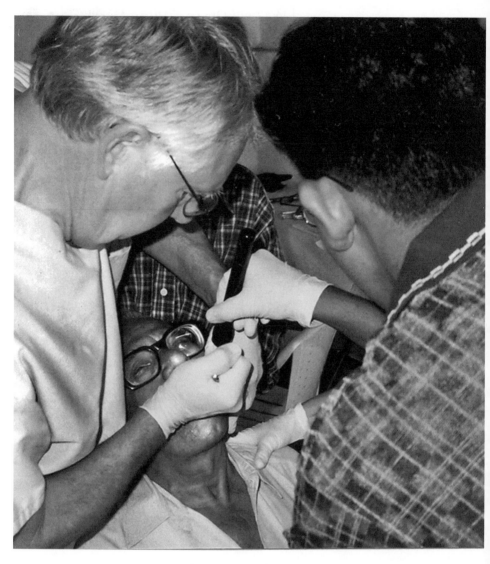

Dr. Nelson, "returning" to India to provide needed dental care for the Indian people that his missionary grandparents had ministered to many years ago.

The Providence
of God

We returned to India because of their great need and we wanted to add dental care. When we were there the first time, it became very apparent that these people desperately needed dental attention in the form of simply pulling diseased infected teeth. We tried to encourage dentists to join our medical group but the dentists we approached were either too busy with their practices, or their families or couldn't afford the money or the time off. It became too late to include a dentist, as we were to leave in just one week and it required more than three weeks to get an Indian visa. We told our host in India that we couldn't get a dentist. We forgot to include God's providential care and plans in our arrangement

I asked for prayer on Sunday in Atascadero Bible Church, my home church, and in my Sunday school class the week before we were to leave for India. "His Healing Hands" was sending a medical team back to India in partnership with Revival Literature Fellowship of India under the leadership of John Ishmael, and also partnering with David Chagall of the cable TV Jewish evangelistic ministry, "The Last Hour." I had learned to always have prayer partners, after my last trip to India. I told them that I wouldn't attempt to go on these trips to the uttermost parts of the world without prayer warriors on their knees praying for our (God's) trip. After teaching my Bible study in Sunday school, a dentist approached me and said, "I wish that I had known that your group was going to India, because I am off this month and I have always wanted to return to India." He had never really been there but his heart was there because his missionary grandparents died there many years ago. They had traveled to India at the turn of the century in 1900 as Christian missionaries. His grandfather died of smallpox and his grandmother stayed in India because of her love of the people. Dr. Nelson had been given old letters written by his grandmother, which he cherished for years. He had "discussed" the issue with God and he decided that he needed to travel to India to see the country where his father was born and his grandparents died. God had been calling him to go to India for years. This sounded very familiar to me.

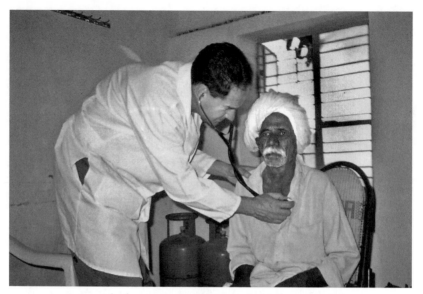

Examíníng an Indían patíent ín Chenaí.

A word of advice: If God calls you, say what Moses, Elijah, Isaiah, and Samuel said. "Here I am Lord." Don't reject God's calling. I felt this same call for a long time before I answered the call. I came to realize that it is an honor, a privilege, and an opportunity to serve God. He will raise up those that He requires to accomplish His will. If we don't respond, He will raise up someone else. Don't miss the blessing. Moses at first was very reluctant and gave excuses. Samuel had to have the call explained to him, but Isaiah jumped at the chance and begged God to "Take me," and said, "Here I am Lord."

Dr. Nelson was now prepared to listen and answer that call of God. We at "His Healing Hands" had been planning this return to India for over one year. Arrangements had been made for visas, airplane tickets, hotels, in-country travel, and church contacts. We had desperately been looking for a dentist to join us, and here he was just five days before our departure. Doctor Nelson was the perfect dentist to go on this trip. He had a lot of past humanitarian missionary dental experience from his many trips to Mexico. He knew what equipment to bring on our journey, and had a special suitcase to carry his portable equipment. He knew what was accomplishable out in the field, and he heard the call and wanted to respond. He was just what the doctor ordered. Over the last five years, hundreds of medical personnel have approached me and praised our medical missionary organization. They say "I would love to go, but". Then they would proceed to give me their many reasons of why they are unable to join us at this time. I have heard all their excuses, and they are all good ones. If they weren't good they wouldn't say them. They miss out on the immense blessing of serving God and doing the very thing we were created to do. As I have said before, it's like the last piece of a puzzle that fits just right and completes the picture. We were too late. It was impossible to get Dr. Nelson a visa, airplane tickets, or make connections half way around the world. It was impractical and foolhardy and pie-in-the-sky thinking to arrange all these plans in a five-day period. However I forgot about the providence of God. When God calls, and you say, "Here I am Lord," then stand back and watch God do the unattainable. He opens door after door and the unexpected occurs. When we are at the end of our finite rope, then God begins to act. God can do all things and nothing is impossible with Him. We finally did what all Christians do when all else fails. At last, we did what we should have done first. We prayed. When will we ever learn? I have to admit; I didn't consider the remote possibility that he would be able to go. Jeff Walker, the president of "His Healing Hands," sent out e-mails for prayer.

Dr. Nelson, our hopeful and faithful dentist called the Indian con-

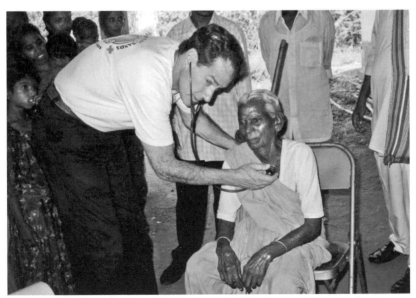

We treated an endless supply of needy Indian patients.

A Christian grammar school in India.

sulate in San Francisco. Apparently, he had more faith in the providential care of God than I did. He relayed to the consulate our humanitarian medical mission and they agreed to provide him a visa in one day if he traveled to San Francisco to their office. This was a privilege only given to ambassadors, and Dr. Nelson was obviously going to be an ambassador for God. He had made himself available to God and he was in the will of God and God honored his statement, "Here I am Lord." He drove four hours up to San Francisco. He spent the entire day there. They were only going to give out a set amount of visas that day due to the load of necessary forms. He was going to have to return the next day, until he told them his story and said, "I think God wants me to go on this trip to India." The secretary to the consulate was a believer and secured another visa for that day.

The next step, he called Singapore Airlines. Our itinerary on Singapore Airlines was from Los Angeles to Taipei to Singapore to New Delhi, but two legs of the trip were completely sold out. Nolan called Air India. Nothing was available. He called other airlines, as he was willing to accept even a circuitous path to our destination. He was willing to go either way around the world, either East or West, since India was half way around the world from Los Angeles. All the doors were closed. We knew it couldn't be done! Again, Dr. Nolan Nelson had this belief that it was God's plan, so he went ahead, got his dental tools out of the garage, sent them off to be sterilized and waited faithfully for God to orchestrate His plan. He stepped out in faith. He decided to remain available and have faith in Jesus Christ; the God of infinite possibilities. He called the airlines the next day but no tickets were attainable at any airlines for any time during our trip schedule. Nothing had opened up.

In talking to the airline ticket agent, he said that it was a shame because our medical missionary team needed a dentist and he was ready to go to India in the name of Jesus. She paused and asked, "Are you a Christian? Are you a believer?" He told her that he was a believer. She told him to hang on while she consulted with her "Supervisor." Nolan waited on the Lord. Miraculously, after this airline ticket agent spoke to her "Supervisor," tickets became available for every leg of the journey from Los Angeles to Taipei to Singapore to New Delhi and all the return legs. Inexplicable he was on all the same flights as the rest of the team and at the same discounted price that was no longer available at this late date. We had all consulted with the right "Supervisor," the great Provider, the wonderful Counselor. The Bible is correct when it states, "All things are possible in Him who strengthens me." We all headed to India to provide medical and dental care to Indian people who never get the opportunity to ever see a medical doctor or a dentist and all in the name of Jesus.

India is crowded, smoggy, and wretchedly poor. It is difficult to breath in Delhi. There is no personal space, and the poverty is a stark testimony to pantheism with each person believing in thousands of gods. This is in sharp contrast to opulent temples, solid inlaid marble mausoleums, one of which is the Taj Mahal, and the desolate populous giving their rupees to Hindu idol gods. But I still love India, because of the loving welcoming Christian people. In every city where we disembarked, these beautiful dear people met us with flowered lays, and always sent us off with flowers and tears in their eyes at our departures. They were waiting for us at the airport, carried our bags, arranged for transportation and lodging, and opened their homes to us for meals that they wouldn't make for themselves or even their children because of the high cost. They are the embodiment of Christians demonstrating hospitality. One of the many blessing of "His Healing Hands" medical missionary organization besides; our humanitarian aid, our encouragement to the people who we care for, being a witness for Jesus Christ, and helping plant new churches; we can come alongside the in-country

The lines of our medical clinics were long, but everyone
waited and received care

indigenous pastors to support them and lift them up in the eyes of their wonderful hospitable people. They give us all they have, even the widow's mite. We come to bless them and they wind up blessing us. We constantly learn from God, His word and His people.

Dr. Nelson treated hundreds of patients. Some of the patients had to be convinced to get his care because of their fear of the unknown, as they had never seen a dentist. During the evenings, we went to the lectures of David Chagal who was discussing the "End Times." We also had an opportunity to give our testimonies during these meetings. The Indian people loved to here Dr. Nelson relating the story of his missionary grandparents who loved India and the Indian people and were willing to devote their very lives to their country. Dr. Nelson accomplished a dream of a lifetime and God used his faithfulness to help the spiritual people of India. Dr. Nelson had brought six hundred ampoules of anesthesia and worried about bringing the correct amount. On the last day of our clinics, he treated the last patient with the five hundredth and ninety-ninth of his six hundred ampoules of anesthesia. He had one left. In God's hand, this was a perfect trip.

While we were in Calcutta, India, we decided to visit Mother Theresa's "Home for the Destitute Dying." This was a tremendously emotional experience. I was not prepared for what I saw and I was not ready for my intense, disturbing, poignant feelings. I have been a doctor for thirty-five years and have seen a lot of horrible illnesses and the results of accidents, "natural diseases," and the effect of man's inhumanity to man, but I wasn't equipped for what I observed. Mother Theresa's "hospice" contained very Spartan surroundings, with the very bare necessities for the Belgian nurses/nuns who cared for the home. These caregivers slept on the floor by choice so as not to take up a patient's bed. They ate very little food, again so as not to take away from the destitute dying. In the main room, on a concrete floor there were one hundred beds with human skeletons, on clean sheets, clothed in diapers with drab blankets to cover some of them. It was dreadfully hot and humid, but there was no smell of feces or urine. In front of me was a scene of defeat and dying, with the smell of death all around. The floor was concrete in order to hose down the human vomit and other secretions. This horrible place of human sufferings and meager surroundings was spotlessly clean. Many of the patients were in a semi-comatose state, breathing with an open mouth to get the last bit of oxygen they could inhale. In stark contrast to this scene, the sisters were smiling, cheerful and joyous.

I spoke with one of the nuns, while she was sponging down one of these emaciated patients to comfort this obviously terminally ill woman. This sister was not only in good spirits, but she exuded joy and a delightful positive attitude in spite of the overwhelming scene of horror. She had been in this home for thirty years, spending the majority of her time in this room, helping these unfortunate street people of Calcutta. This contrast between dying skeletons and this joyous nun was too much for me to absorb or handle emotionally, but it was real and necessary. My feelings came upon me in rapid-fire succession of sadness, compassion, guilt, horror, confusion, and misunderstanding.

In the past, I have been praised for my medical service to the underprivileged poor and for our organization, "His Healing Hands." We are a short-term medical missionary group who donate our time, money and expertise, but we return to our plush homes in the United States with showers, air conditioning, good meals and family ties. These nuns were home, with no end in sight except their own death. They were joyous, blissful, and enthusiastic. There was an obvious contentment and emotional calmness in their very demeanor. They had a vision of

Our Indian medical team with our hosts in
front of the Taj Mahal

the temporal nature of their life on earth and their focus was on heaven with an eye on caring for those in need here on earth. I will never forget this scene of suffering coupled with the amazing, cheerful care and attitude of these astonishing nuns. These nuns were visibly filled with the presence of God and they were concentrating on God and not themselves. I don't believe their actions could be sustained without God. I saw God in their faces and their actions. My faith was increasing through prayer, God's providence and His grace in allowing me to be of service to His people. These caregivers considered it to be an honor and opportunity to serve God and not an obligation. The inspiration of service for me had been there but now I was beginning to understand the true meaning of service, with a need to focus on God and not on myself. I had wanted more faith from God, but it wasn't about me. It was about God, His people, my witness in representing Him as His ambassador, and my relationship to Him. I was doing medical missions for a while by now but I had a lot to learn about being of service to God and His people. Service is admirable especially when it is performed by a cheerful giver, and to be effective and to please God at the same time it must be accompanied by the joy, peace, and love of God. When you visit Mother Teresa's Hospice, you can't avoid thinking about your own mortality. We will all die eventually, but we try to live by putting this fact into the back of our subconscious thoughts. We must and should

David Chagall giving an evening lecture
on "The Last Days."

live with the daily conscious thought of dying. I am convinced that we cannot properly live in this world without a daily booster shot called death. Without God, we are truly the destitute dying, but with God, death is a beginning of glory and not an ending of being impoverished. Death is not a depressive, sullen thought if you are a believer in the God of the Bible and you have the assurance of salvation. I will always be able to conjure up the image of that Belgian nun whose peace and joy permeates her very being and reflects the glory of her God.

My faith was increasing by being with God's people, relying on prayer, understanding the providence of God and being in His will. I thought that I understood service but I came to realize that I was actually serving myself and not God and His people as these sincere sisters demonstrated. Faith was turning out to be more than I had grasped and God was fulfilling His side of the covenant and all I had to do was have an open mind and heart and be available to Him. The experience at Mother Teresa's "Home for the Destitute Dying" was very emotional. I was finding out how emotional and how intimate, as my relationship with God was evolving.

My daughter Faith at the Great Wall of China

Christianity is not a Religion but an Intimate Relationship

A fter my initial medical missionary trip to Haiti, I wanted to continue to serve God and the poor in His name. I called many different organizations but they were all geared for long term commitments and they couldn't accommodate doctors in private practice. It occurred to me that there were thousands of highly qualified medical personnel willing to donate their time on a limited basis. These doctors, like myself, had a desire to serve but had families with young children, limited funds with high expenses and large mortgages, and only had short periods of time available to serve. I wanted to find a way to make medical missions available to all the people who wanted to serve but were not "full" time missionaries. Over the years, I have met thousands of caring, loving, humanitarian minded, Americans who wanted to help the less fortunate peoples of the world. As the most powerful country in the world, we have been doing humanitarian work all over the world without regard to race, religion, or nationality, since our inception as a nation. A tremendous example of this is our massive financial aid to Indonesia after the Tsunami disaster, including the United States military men and women, and civilian voluntary organizations such as our group of "His Healing Hands." From personal experience, I can state that many of the Islamic people didn't want our help at first but they "warmed up" to our compassionate medical care. It is sometimes difficult to treat a nation that is anti-American but we as Americans don't allow other peoples prejudice to affect our humanitarian aid. For the believer, the world is both a battlefield and a mission field. We are called to go into the world and share with the unbelieving world, the good news of forgiveness after repentance and the reward of eternal life with God. Jesus also said that we are not of the world but we are to remain in the world and the world will hate us as they hated Him. How then can we accomplish His will in a Jesus hating world when we represent Him? It can only be accomplished through the Holy Spirit and His repeated filling when we are in His will. Americans want to help and I felt that there must be an avenue for people like me to serve.

Our Christian nation guarantees religious freedom for all religions, but this is not true of non-Christian nations. Islamic countries or communist countries don't tolerate other religions such as Christianity or Judaism. There is a movement in the United States to take all Christian symbols off all government buildings and insignias. Our government was founded on Judaic-Christian ethics and principles, and these foundations have protected all its citizens. The government doesn't have to promote Christianity but why should they try to destroy the principles and institutions that have worked to protect all of us? It is foolhardy to try to dismantle institutions like the Boys and Girls Club, or the Salvation Army, or the Y.M.C.A., which have helped to develop strong American values. When our group, "His Healing Hands" applied for visas to go to Pakistan in the Himalayan Mountains after their major earthquake, our visas were titled the "Islamic state of Pakistan," and the only reason we were allowed to enter the country as a Christian medical missionary organization was because of their dire need of help. When I was treating one of the local mountain people, I asked him if he was glad that we as Americans were giving him aid. He said, "when our bellies are full we don't want American food but when we are hungry we will accept your help." We, as American Christians, are ready and available to help all peoples and in fact we help more Islamic people then any other religious or ethnic groups. I knew that there were more American doctors like myself who would love to help underprivileged people in third world nations if they could treat them for short periods of time under the proper conditions. This idea came to fruition by a series of incidents that I believe were orchestrated by God in His providential care.

I was teaching an adult Sunday school class, when I approached an extremely godly, bright and insightful woman named, Iris, with my idea. She had a son and a grandson who were both missionaries with "Campus Crusade for Christ." Iris advised me to talk with her son who at times had attended the class when he was in town visiting her. He had been a missionary to Guam, Canada, and Mongolia, and he had many contacts with missionaries around the world. He said that he could get me in contact with the right person, but I wasn't prepared with the speed or method of this contact nor the results nor the destination. Three weeks later, I was on a United Airline plane to Beijing, China to meet a man named, Victor, whom I had never met, and who had never even spoken with me. It dawned on me while I was on this eleven hour flight, that all I had to do was find one Asian man named, Victor, in the city of Beijing where I couldn't even read the signs in Chinese characters. I quickly learned that when you pray in God's will, you had better be prepared to act on the answer.

It all started with my first e-mail on a computer that I had bought for my children. I was computer illiterate and didn't know about communicating via e-mail. A man named, Victor, from Singapore invited me to help start a new medical clinic in a remote part of southern China. I was overwhelmed and amazed. He told me to send my passport to a certain address to arrange for a Chinese visa and airline tickets and meet him in Beijing, China at a designated time and place. This was either a test of faith or of my stupidity and gullibility. My contact from

Our medical team; a pharmacist, 2 nurses,
3 doctors and translators

my Sunday school class assured me that Victor was a long time vice-president of "Campus Crusade for Christ," in charge of the Asian division. This was all new to me, and a bit intimidating. My desire was to serve and I had prayed about this service, but the answers were not what I had expected. Looking back at my expectations, I'm not sure what I anticipated. First I was "sent" to Haiti, and now to communist China. I guess I was thinking of the French Riviera, but that's not where the needs were. My wife and children were worried about my plans and I didn't know what to expect or how to reassure them. I had prayed for more faith and it was surely being tested. My upbringing on the streets of New York City had taught me to handle many situations and I decided that it was time to take the challenge. I had secret fortifications; the love of God and the security of being in His will.

I responded to Victor's e-mail. I sent in my passport, paid for my tickets, revamped my office schedule, and vexed my family about this unknown venture. I left for China on a Friday afternoon. I drove to Los Angeles Airport and boarded a plane at midnight. I "lost" a day after crossing the International Date Line and arrived in Beijing on Sunday. Victor had instructed me not to talk to any one after disembarking and not to exchange any money. He said that, there were counterfeiters and I could get into trouble with the authorities at the airport. At this time, China was not as open as it is today. He told me to go directly to the kiosk of the Movenpick Hotel and give them my name. I followed his instructions. No one spoke English but a porter was carrying my suitcase away and I just followed him to the hotel van. He drove through the streets of Beijing. Although, I lived in New York City for twenty-five years, this was the most crowded, busy, overwhelming city that I had ever seen. I arrived at the hotel and went to the lobby still following my bag. I was tired, apprehensive and I felt extremely vulnerable. Mercifully, the hotel clerk spoke perfect English. I told him my name and he instructed me to go to a large banquette room. I opened the door and there were well over fifty people in what seemed to be some sort of lecture. A short smiling, joyous man approached me and said, "welcome Dr. Frankel." I breathed a sigh of relief. Victor had a seat waiting for me by his side. The adventure was just starting.

In that room were very important people. Besides Victor; the vice president of "Campus Crusade for Christ" in Asia, there was the head of the worldwide Jesus Film Project and a group of very wealthy American Christian donors, and yet they treated me as if I was special. Actually, Victor treats every one as if they were the most important person in the room. He is one of the most efficient, capable, educated (a doctorate plus two master degrees), bold and yet humble man that I have ever met. One of the benefits to going on these medical missionary trips is that I have met some of the greatest humans on the planet. They may not be heads of governments or kings or stars as the world judges, but I know by their words and actions of giving and receiving love and their care for fellow human beings that they are the noblest of us all. You could feel the energy in that banquette room. You could feel the love. You could sense the Spirit of God. These experiences and relationships have blessed my soul. I was learning that there was more to this development of my faith then I had realized. Faith comes from God but we are involved in this process of developing this faith, if we are yielded to the Spirit of God and allow that Spirit to take over the reins of our life. I was learning by seeing and hearing and fellowshipping with God's people. I learned in that meeting that this group of believers was planning to develop, build, and fund "the Agape Love center" in southern China, which would contain a medical clinic. I was given the honor to help set up and staff this clinic. We finished our meeting and went to bed to be rested for another airplane trip followed by a three-hour van ride in the morning. Before falling asleep, I lay in bed pinching myself because I couldn't believe that I was in Communist China on a mission from God, as a Jewish, Christian, American medical doctor. I was exhausted but I was eager, expectant, excited, anxious, and my anticipation of our approaching "adventure" was almost overwhelming. I couldn't believe that I had initiated this journey; or Did I? Years later, Victor told me while reminiscing about our past trips that he had prayed for an American doctor to contact him in order to set up this clinic in China. The day after his prayer, after the inquiry of my Sunday School attendee, I presented "my" idea to him. I now believe that my medical missionary career was initiated by Victor's prayer and orchestrated by God.

The next day, with my new associates, we headed for Southeastern, China to eventually arrive in an unpronounceable province. We were headed to a small town by Chinese standards of seven hundred thousand inhabitants. Everything looked gray without color. There were few trees and no birds. It seemed that under Mao Tse Tung, the government felt that the birds were eating the people's food and they tried to eradicate the bird population. I guess they were not worried about endangering species. In the Pacific Northwest of the United States, we destroyed the entire logging industry over six pairs of spotted owls. In this communistic government without common rights or freedoms for the people, they needed to feed their population in contrast to our Christian nation that now feels animals are more important then humans. In the city, they had a lot of ongoing building projects as if the government expected a new and vibrant economy was going to arise in this town. The streets were wide and there were hundreds of street sweepers on rickshaws. The people wore identical gray clothing with identical hats, and were very busy driving strange looking diesel trucks,

Typical Chinese city, with modern buildings, wide streets for future commerce and old peasants going to market

riding hundreds of bicycles, intermingled with donkey carts overloaded with all kinds of farm produce. I had read that China was emerging as a world economic power and the scene before my eyes verified that statement. We arrived at a church compound in the middle of this bustling city. I had previously read that churches were illegal in China, and here was a large church with a lit up cross on the top of the steeple in the middle of the city, seen by every one. This miraculous site was the first of many "miracles" that I was to observe. The beginning of this church,

Every seat was filled in the Chinese church, supported by American missionary donors

which is attended by a standing room only crowd of about six thousand poor Chinese farmers, is a fascinating story in itself.

The pastor of the church was a small, petit, eighty-five pound, female ball of fire, with unlimited energy and the faith to match. Upon our arrival we were directed into a tiny dingy wet room where the pastor was busy baptizing over three hundred and fifty new believers. In China, many of the pastors are women because many of the men of God have been martyred. This pastor came from a line of eight pastors and her grandfather had died in jail. She was very bright and she wanted to be a businesswoman and certainly not a pastor. As a devoted Christian, she attended the best Christian college that her family could afford, which was a Christian seminary. She excelled and was number one in her class.

During the Tianamen square incident in Beijing, many of the bright, young future upcoming communist leaders were very disenchanted to see army tanks running over their people. In order to calm down these young scholars, the communist leadership went to her seminary to find the brightest student to speak to these future leaders. . They chose this future reluctant pastor.

She wasn't sure what to do. Was this a scam to discover her religious beliefs and weed her out of school or worse to imprison her like her grandfather? She consulted with wise Christian counselors and prayed. She decided to trust God with her life. Genuine faith is exhibited by putting it all on the line and relying only on God. This young Christian women spent four hours locked in a room with one-hundred, bright young future communist leaders and when they emerged from that cloistered room all the these future leaders accepted Jesus as their Savior. Not just ninety-eight or ninety-nine but all of them. This was a miraculous strange breathtaking event and its awesome implications did not get past this young woman. What did this mean? What was the inference? What should she do and what next? She spoke with her mother and told her that she wanted to be a businesswoman but how could she ignore this? Her mother told her that when she was born, she had dedicated her infant daughter's life to God just as Hanna in the Bible had dedicated Samuel's life to God. This young daughter asked her mother why she hadn't told her of this before the evangelistic incident? Her wise godly mother replied," I wanted you to discover this on your own in God's time." Our pastor's life was changed in a twinkling of an eye. This want-to-be businesswoman was on the road to serving God full time in the pastorate. She obeyed the calling of God. Several years ago I asked her, "How many baptisms have you performed in your ten year ministry?" She told me "over forty-thousand." This is obviously a woman called and used by God. I was in the presence of one of the noblest of all of God's people. It is easy for a believer such as myself to be humble in the presence of such as these.

Mass baptism of 1500 Chinese believers

We arrived at her church (you may have noticed that I have avoided using her name for obvious reasons), on a Saturday and viewed some of the three hundred and fifty baptisms that the pastor and the elders were performing that day. The next day, Sunday was just as amazing. The church service was scheduled for nine in the morning but the peasants started arriving at five in the morning and I'm told that many of them started from their brick and mud huts the night before. They arrived by donkey carts, rickshaws, motorbikes, pedal bikes, taxis cabs and by foot after walking for many long hours. The church service was standing room only. They were all clean, wearing their best clothes, carrying Chinese Bibles or portions of Bibles on old worn pieces of paper and they sang unto the Lord with obvious joy and awe and reverence. This service lasted four hours and they wanted more and never lost their concentration. It was the first time that I had sung hymns in English while listening to the same song in another language. It was inspiring. It was the same songs. It was the same God, the one and only true God. Only Jesus could have brought all our diversity together for the same purpose of worship, praise, proclaiming, and listening to the word of God and to glorify Him. Unlike us, these people had suffered for their right to worship. They had made an unbelievable effort to get to church to worship God. They had risked all they had including their very lives.

Bicycles, the main transportation for the churchgoers.

I have read the Bible many times, sat through many sermons, and even taught Sunday school for many years, but now I was learning for the first time the intimacy, the emotional, and the truly personal relationship between God and His people. These astonishing people without speaking my language made the Bible alive and real to me. Since I didn't understand the sermon in Chinese, my mind wondered back in time to the Upper Room when Jesus tried to strengthen His disciples after shocking them with the thought of His leaving. He told them that they could not follow Him at this time, and He gave them a "new" commandment. "A new commandment I give to you, that you love one another, even as I have loved you. By this all men will know that you are my disciples." This commandment really wasn't new since the Jewish "Old Testament" says to love your neighbor as yourself, but Jesus made it personal and sacrificial. He showed his love sacrificially by giving up His earthly life for us. Think of what God the Father asked of God the Son; to give up some of His divine attributes to take on human form and sacrifice for a people who would reject and torture him and kill Him. It is as if, we were asked to die for a bunch of cockroaches that would hate us and kill us for trying to save them. If we think this is stretching the point, we must realize that the gulf between man and God is wider and deeper than the gap between man and any beast.

These poor Chinese peasant workers exhibited this love for one another and were truly His disciples. I came to China to help set up a medical clinic and to teach these people, but they were teaching me about the intimate relationship between Jesus and His people and their relationship to one another. Jesus goes on to tell His disciples that He is

The crowd in the waiting room of our clinic. George, my brother-in-law, playing the clarinet, was great for Sino-American relations

in the Father and the Father is in Him and that He is in all of us. Later, He describes another Comforter who will dwell in us, and relates to them that they are children of God. Think of the personal intimacy of these relationships. Think of the supernatural relationship, we as believers have with God living within us. The Christian life is an emotional, personal, intimate, supernatural life. It is Jesus' life lived out in every believer and these "rich" people were living out this life. I was stunned and shaken. This was beyond anything I had expected. All that is Jesus is available to us, if we make all that we are available to Him.

I spent the rest of that week living with these people, treating them medically with my single bag of medicines and planning to return to a medical clinic that was to be built by my American benefactor colleagues. It didn't seem possible but within one year the clinic building was enclosed but not completed and I planned my return.

Pharmacy of a Satellite Clinic of "His Healing Hands,"
created in a church in China

Patients signing up for a "His Healing Hands" medical
clinic in China

God Raises up
Workers for the Harvest

I intended to return on my own, gather up sample medicine with the help of the drug detail people that come to my private office and get some donated medicines promised to me through the local hospital where I practiced. My office nurse went to the hospital to pick up these promised medicines and the chief pharmacist of the hospital followed her back to my office. Jeff Walker knocked on my door and asked me where I was taking the medicine. When I told him, China to do medical missionary work, he asked if he could come along with me. God had sent me a fellow worker without my own inquiry or request. We sat and talked for hours and we agreed that we could see more patients with two bags of medicines and two sets of healing hands. God in His providential care was orchestrating the beginning of something that I had never dreamed or anticipated. The fellowship of the believers is a powerful tool in the hands of God. Each of us has some type of spiritual gift of the Holy Spirit and God had just multiplied those gifts in fellowship between Jeff and myself. Jeff arranged for his passport and Chinese visa and we headed off to southern China. Now there were two of us and where two or three are gathered together, there He is in their midst. We drove to Los Angeles Airport and arrived in China via Tokyo, Japan. Our hosts picked us up, after having to explain to the Chinese custom officials, why two Americans were bringing in one hundred and forty pounds of various medicines. They were about to detain us and confiscate our medicines. We both silently prayed and without warning they changed their minds and abruptly demanded that we move on and we gladly thanked God and were received by our hosts. It seemed that God was walking before us and preparing the way. It reminded me of the children of Israel, being led in the Sinai Desert by the cloud by day and the fire by night. My Sunday school classes and biblical stories were starting to be lived out in the experiences that God had set before me. This has subsequently happened to us during many of our trips and we have learned to pray in advance and totally rely on God. There is nothing "magical" about prayer but it is our part in our relationship to God the Father through Jesus the Son. God wants us to pray and rely on

Him and enhance our personal relationship to Him. We were now learning together. It seems when you are on the mission field and thinking only of being in God's will, He does miraculous things.

We arrived in our church compound to find a new beautiful building by Chinese standards but we were in for a surprise. The building was only a shell and it was in December in eastern China and it was literally freezing cold. When we started to see patients the next day,

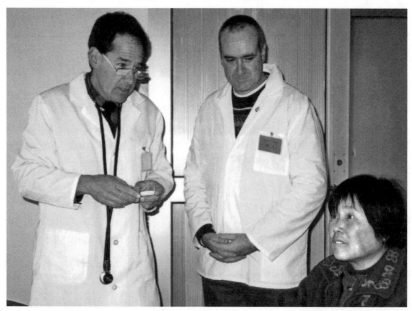

Jeff and I treating a Chinese peasant woman

our hosts gave us hot water to drink. At first we were amazed that this drink was not even tea but we were so cold and we needed to have our hands free to examine the patients and we were glad to have this hot water and it was necessary and delicious under the circumstances. After our long journey and the change of time coupled with jetlag, we were exhausted. We greeted our hosts as best we could and slept in our clothes and awakened to an endless line of patients who started to line up at five in the morning.

Jeff set up a makeshift pharmacy and I started to examine the patients. The two of us treated four times the number of patients than one doctor alone could have treated. We were much more efficient together and we mutually enhanced each other's care. At first, I was surprised to observe that these Chinese farmers were all overweight until I realized that they all had multiple layers of clothes. The record for layers was nine. We started to wear multiple layers as well. We were learning from our patients. Since some of these patients were very short in stature, I had to kneel down to listen to their heart. I later found out that it was unusual for Chinese doctors to touch their patients. Many of the patients told me their diagnosis that they had been given by Chinese doc-

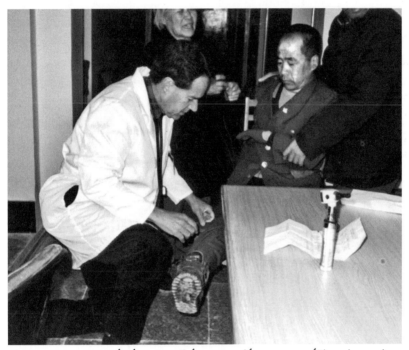

Here I am examining a Chinese policeman with a leg ulcer who I later discovered was diabetic.

tors. I questioned them further and found out that all these different diagnosis were made only by taking the patient's pulse with no other examination or diagnostic tests. When I kneeled down to examine the patients, one of my Chinese translators would attempt to place a pillow under my knee. This kneeling down was very insignificant to me but I later found out that it had a huge affect on the people.

That night at dinner at the church makeshift dinning room, all the Chinese staff kept pointing to us and giving us looks of admiration and broadly smiling at us. One of our translators related to me that we had made a great impression on all the people. I figured it was our good care and efficiency, but it was something completely different. The word had spread that when I examined patients, the tall American Christian doctor was not only willing to touch them, but kneel down on the floor before them. This simple act that I performed to be able to listen to their hearts and save my back from repeatedly bending over, was interpreted as being a wonderful act of humility. These unassuming, modest, unpretentious, poor Chinese peasants were the humble ones and this simple act was very important to them and very convicting to me. I thought about Jesus washing the dusty feet of the disciples. He did this just after they had discussed among themselves, who in the midst of them would be the greatest in the kingdom of God. Jesus even washed the feet of Judas, who He knew was about to betray Him. Jesus said, "For I am gentle and humble at heart." Our culture thinks to be humble or meek is to be insignificant, unworthy, spineless and small. It doesn't mean that at all. It means to stoop low and serve others. There is no way that you can fake humility. You can fake love. You can fake patience. You can fake acceptance, or tolerance, or wealth, but you can't fake humility. If you try to show humility, it is pride. You can't lecture on how to be humble or write a book on humility or talk about being humble or achieving humility. Humility is not thinking less of yourself. It is not thinking of yourself at all. When you have humility, you don't know it or think about it. I may have been helping these people medically, but these simple peasants were convicting me and helping me get closer to God. Their love of God was as simple as a child's faithful, dependent love. Since this quality of humility is the least obvious quality a man can realize he has, it must come from the Spirit of God. I had come to help and I was being helped. This scenario has repeated itself on all of our medical missionary trips. My Christian walk was helped more than the patients were helped by my medical care.

I learned another principal about humility in a very humorous way when Jeff and I were taken out to dinner at a fancy Chinese restaurant hosted by one of the few Chinese benefactors of the church. Our hosts were very grateful for our care of their people and they wanted to take us out to dinner and give us the best that they could provide. The restaurant prepared Chinese delicacies to honor us. One of these

Chinese delicacies served to honor me. The dish in the middle was full of live, moving worms

delicacies was a bowl of raw, live silk worms. Jeff and I looked at each other and knew that this "dish" had been especially prepared to honor us. I swallowed, gathered up my courage, smiled and ate this "treat," as did Jeff. We all bowed and laughed heartily. I guess, we had passed the test. Our hosts ate the remainder of the bowl of worms but I declined any more of these delicacies. I realized that humility is being willing to receive as well as give without embarrassment, and not be afraid of being vulnerable and show trust. A Christian is not only called to love but to let others love him. It also demonstrates that humility is not a sign of weakness, as it took all my inner strength to eat that worm.

When I made my initial "deal" with God to do medical missionary work and increase my faith, I thought it would be a simple, sudden, spiritual awakening. It has turned out to be much more. I am realizing that it is a process that involves my relationship to God, my relationship to His body of believers, my compassion for the lost of this world and my own feelings about myself. Faith includes; prayer, the knowledge of God's providence and sovereignty, God's word, wise counselors and fellowship, my availability and humility, and the intimacy of God the Father, God the Son, and the Holy Spirit residing in me. God was moving in my life and teaching me, and I knew that I must continue to say, "Here I am Lord".

The pastor of this church spent as much time with us as she could spare, as she was extremely busy in taking care of all her other churches. She related to us that for the past ten years, she had planted and

Overcrowded village church, with open windows, in spite of the freezing cold, so the people outside could hear the service.

was actively pastoring three hundred churches with an average attendance of one thousand each. This unassuming, caring, modest delightful servant of God was ministering to three hundred thousand poor Chinese peasants in the body of Christ in a cheerful, joyous, and meek manner. She didn't have a glitzy radio or television ministry and she was not supported by wealthy, important donors. She was doing what God had called her to do. She reminded me of a type of John the Baptizer, who came to do a specific job and did it and then got out of the way, so Jesus could increase while John decreased.

I spent a day with her going to several of these churches. Upon approaching these churches on the narrow streets of various Chinese hamlets, the villagers lined the streets, peered in the car windows with beaming faces, and clapped their hands. They were honoring Jesus through this ambassador of God. It was very cold but in these little churches, the windows were left wide open so the people outside the church, who couldn't fit into these little buildings, could hear the pastor give a brief sermon and encourage them. They hung on her every word. While I was in her company, I felt as if I was in the first century, traveling on a missionary trip with the Apostle Paul. By the end of the day after visiting five churches, we arrived back at the main church compound after dark.

A "home" church we visited in a remote village in China

I was exhausted and was given a dinner of vegetables and rice with the other church workers, but the pastor was nowhere to be found. I asked about her and was told that she was practicing with the church choir. She was a woman of inexhaustible energy and strength. Her excitement and enthusiasm for God carried her through grueling days. This setting in the third world of communist China really was like the book of Acts in the first century with missionary journeys, house prayer meetings and many new followers of Jesus. The only element that was missing was the miracles and I was about to find out about them.

I have already chronicled how the pastor was called by God, to lead these people, but how did a large church in the middle of this town with a lighted cross on it's roof for everyone to see, come into being in athe- istic communist China? When the pastor graduated from seminary, she returned to her hometown to set up churches and evangelize the poor. She grew up with the mayor and all the communist city officials and they all respected her honesty and intelligence. The church was com- prised mostly of the working poor farmers but one of the wives of one of the communist officials came to her church and was saved. She told her hairdresser about this wonderful pastor and soon all the hairdress- ers in the beauty parlor were believers. In China, only wealthy women or the communist leaders wives could afford to go to a hair salon. When a woman has her hair done, it takes several hours and the clients are a captive audience, sitting in a chair discussing the events and the topics of the day. One of these women was the wife of the controlling general of the entire province. She became a believer and an attendee of the church and a personal friend of the pastor. She told the other believers that her husband had been diagnosed with terminal cancer, which had spread, all over his body and both eastern and western medicine could do no more for him. They prayed for him and his wife asked the pastor to pray for his cure. He was invited to go to church. The general didn't believe in God and refused. He continued to get worse and was close to death. His wife continued to beg him to let the pastor pray over him. He was so weak that he finally gave in and agreed but only during the darkness of night and in his home. The pastor was not sure if this was a scheme to arrest her and disband the believers. She prayed and fellowshipped with her wise Christian counselors and decided that this was being orchestrated by the providence of God. This was a major step of faith for the pastor as she remembered her martyred grandfather. She went to the general's house in the cover of night and witnessed and prayed for him. The next day, he was fully cured; no pain, no nausea, no shortness of breath and he felt strong and was able to eat for the first time in two weeks. He told the pastor that she could have a piece of land to build a church in the middle of the city. He became a believer although a "closet" secretive Christian and he protected the church, the believers and the pastor. It seems that God can use disease, pain and even communism to achieve His will. . All through the Bible, God uses incidences of sin, unrighteousness and disasters to turn events and people around as a witness for good. God is never the author of sin, but He can affect the outcome of man's falling short of the glory of God to advance His kingdom. The worst thing that man has ever done to God is to crucify Him. The best thing that God has ever done for man is to convert this sin into the resurrection. He is the God of everyone even Chinese generals.

When the church grew and they needed a bigger place to meet, they chose a vacant lot next to the church and invited all the city dignitaries to attend a ceremony. Since they all knew and respected the pastor and because the communist constitution touts freedom of religion, they agreed to attend. It didn't hurt that she had the backing of the general of the province. In southern China, they grow delicious apples and offer them at ceremonies. The mayor of the town was listening to the pastor speak and she asked him if the church could purchase this vacant lot next to the church. The congregation didn't have any money

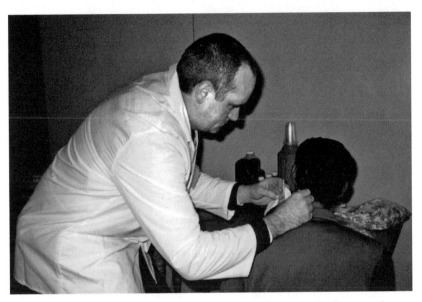

Jeff Walker, our pharmacist and president of His Healing Hands, caring for a peasant's neck wound.

but they had a lot of faith in the God of the Bible. The mayor picked up a very crisp, hard apple and teasingly told the pastor that he would give the land to the church if she could split the apple down the middle with her bare hands. She is a very bold, believing, faithful servant of the Lord Most High and in front of the entire crowd; she dropped to her knees to pray cupping the apple in her hands. She prayed out loud to God that His will be done and she opened her cupped hands to reveal a perfectly split beautiful apple and she offered one half to the mayor and displayed the other half to the gathering. The mayor was stunned and granted the land to the church without a fee. A fruit had been used in the Bible in the past with different results but when righteousness is involved, the outcome will be in accordance with God's will.

These Chinese doctors were my helpers and translators

Jeff and I had never experienced anything like this in our entire Christian walk. We were deeply affected by these people and their stories and our lives would never be the same. They were the real deal and God was moving among them and using them to disciple this huge nation. That week, we treated about one thousand patients and administered to the church staff as well. We truly became family and Jeff and I have gone back there at least twice yearly and we are planning a permanent "His Healing Hands" clinic staffed by a local indigenous doctor, who we will train and supply with medicines and equipment. Sometimes in the United States, you get the feeling that the gospel is not moving forward. However in China, The Holy Spirit is as active as recorded in the first century in the book of Acts. On the plane home, Jeff was very quiet and then told me that he had decided to move his entire family to that little city in China and become the administrator of the hospital. God was stirring the pot of our lives. When we arrived home our anxious families were relieved but they were in for a big surprise.

There is Not Enough Time in a Day But God Will Redeem the Time

God was increasing my faith with prayer, through His word, through wise counselors, through His providence, and the fellowship of His people. Originally, I thought faith was a simple one step concept but I wasn't thinking spiritually. When we came home from China, we started to learn about stewardship and how it is tied to faith. When Christians hear about stewardship, they immediately think that someone wants their money. All organizations need money and of course "His Healing Hands" requires money as well, but we need something more critical. We need people to serve. The harvest is plentiful but the workers are few. Jeff was on fire and he told his family, his wife and two children, to sell the house, quit their jobs and get ready to move to China. In his enthusiasm for God's calling, he dropped a bomb on his family. He had gotten a vision by serving in China, but they had not experienced what he had encountered. After the dust had cleared, his wife, his children and even his parents agreed to accompany him back to China to participate in a medical mission. His wife is a registered nurse, his son is interested in pharmacy school, his daughter is now our mission organizer and in charge of our African division, his father is a computer expert and his mother is extremely helpful in all aspects of hospitality and encouragement. His family went to China and they understood Jeff's passion, and Jeff came to understand something else. He learned that bringing our children on medical missionary trips not only expanded their horizons but also stretched their Christian walk. He also realized that we need to form a medical missionary organization to help others see God's evangelical plan, using medicine as a tool, which would enable us to go to countries that usually don't allow Christian groups to aid their people. This understanding changed our entire direction, as we appreciated that we could multiply ourselves and thereby have a greater effect on advancing God's plan. Jeff and I discussed this, prayed about it, and decided to form a nonprofit humanitarian medical organization that was open to all people that had a desire to follow God's will or just wanted to contribute to the poor and discarded peoples of the world. In addition, we decided to encourage non-believers to come with us as a witness to them, without compromising our core beliefs. Most Christian organizations require that the participants make a profession of faith. All our directors and leaders have made this profession of faith, but we accept all our other workers without regard to their beliefs. There is obviously a danger in doing this, however, every soul won for God is worth the risk. This was exhibited in one of our trips to Mexico.

From left to right: Dr Gonzales (director of Baja hospital), Dr. Kuntz (a urologist), and Dr. Sima (an Orthopedic surgeon) in San Vincente, Baja, Mexico

I had developed a relationship with the medical social service department in San Vincente, Baja, California, and "His Healing Hands" went on a medical missionary trip through Atascadero Bible Church. A Catholic urologist and a non-believing orthopedist joined me in this humanitarian endeavor. While driving down to Baja, the orthopedist asked me the million-dollar question that all evangelical Christians yearn to hear. He knew me as a colleague and had heard my Christian opinions on a social basis. He told me that he admired my faith and assurance of salvation and wished he could have that type of faith. He said that if he did have that type of real, authentic faith, he would become a believer and his anxiety about eternity would be squelched. For three hours, I witnessed to both doctors and answered a lot of questions. The orthopedist asked me about my testimony and how I can be so certain that

Jesus is God. I described my experiences, told him about the miracles of Jesus, His fulfilled prophecies and the eyewitnesses to His death and resurrection. I suggested that he should read the Bible and pray that God will reveal Himself to him. All he had to do while reading the Bible was to have an open mind. The urologist has been a Catholic believer all his life with a love and respect for God and His servants. He rarely talked about God, but when he did, you could feel the love and it was obvious that he was a believer in the Lord Jesus. He was the founder of the Flying Samaritans local Central Coast of California chapter and has done humanitarian work his entire medical career. His Flying Samaritan chapter was inactive for several years but this trip stimulated him to reenergize the chapter, which is now bigger than ever. He has continued to serve in his capacity as president of the local chapter and now does it in the name of Jesus while he has become more verbal about his service. Two months later, the orthopedic surgeon was baptized and the urologist has been on many of our missionary trips and has led a surgical team to Peru. We have learned to be better stewards of our time and God has multiplied our ministry.

When I tell others about our trips and our need of medical personnel, especially doctors, they all say the same thing. "I admire your work and I wish that I could go with you and maybe someday, but I can't now. I can't afford to leave my practice. I have small children. I have school loans and a mortgage. I can't afford the cost of a trip and if I could take the time off, my wife wants to take a vacation." These are all good excuses; but they're still excuses. All excuses are good ones or else we wouldn't give them. I feel badly for these people, not because of the excuses but because these good, well intentioned people miss out on the blessings. We all understand that if you want to do something, you have to first decide to do it and then make it happen. We all have a certain amount of time on earth and we must be good stewards of the time given to us by God. The pastor in China did a lot more than I could ever do in a day and yet she seemed to have more time. The Bible says redeem the time and therefore it is possible. Jesus fulfilled His mission on earth completely and He never appeared to be rushed. We live in a very fast paced, busy society and we spent a lot of time spinning our wheels. If I can serve with my demanding schedule of a medical practice, being on call, running a ranch and farm, teaching a Bible study and raising three children, in addition to going on four to six missionary trips a year, anyone can do it. It only takes a decision, and God will redeem the time for us, if we are good stewards of the life that He has given us. It is actually His time.

This stewardship also is involved with our spiritual gifts of which the Bible says, we all have at least one. When I made a decision to consider my opportunity to serve God, I had to decide, how in the world could God use me? Was it possible, and what could I offer? Should I go to language school, join a Christian group as a full time missionary, move my family to another country, or go back to school and become a seminary student? These life changing, daunting tasks didn't seem appropriate at my stage of life. Then I realized that God could use me just as I am, based on my current positions, experience, relationships, and educational status. I have been a family practice doctor for thirty-five years and taught a Bible study at different times for over twenty years. I grew up on the streets of a big city without possessions but with American opportunities. I have raised three Christian children and have been married for almost thirty years. I have a B.S., an M.D., an M.S., and an honorary doctorate of Divinity. Surely I have had enough schooling to last a lifetime, and if I have a Spiritual gift, I want to start to use it for God's glory in His service.

I opened up my Bible to the section on Spiritual gifts and went down the list. Did I possess the message of wisdom or knowledge? My wife said, "No." How about the gift of faith? I have already discussed my need for more faith. Did I possess the gift of serving, or leadership, or encouragement? I would like to think this but I know a lot of people who have a lot more of these gifts than me. I don't have miraculous powers, the gift of prophecy, or the ability to speak in tongues or any other language beside English. But there it was, staring me in the face; the gift of healing, mercies, and teaching. I didn't have to modify or adjust or revise my personality or vocation or my desires. I am a doctor, a teacher, and I'm comfortable in big cities with underprivileged people. All I had to do was utilize my experiences and abilities given to me by God. That's the formula. Just employ the gifts and talents you already possess. These skills were originally developed to advance God's kingdom, and not for my own agenda. When you use these capabilities for that purpose, you will be amazed at the outcome.

I love to treat patients in my office practice, and I like the average, mundane, treatable diseases. Most doctors find complex, difficult, perplexing medical cases irresistible, whether they are treatable or not. I hate untreatable, incurable, terminal diseases, no matter how intellectually challenging or stimulating. I don't remember the names of my patients that have died. I am sure this is a protective mechanism and my avoidance of the pain of losing friendly, affable, and reliant relationships. I love the feeling of helping others and seeing the joy on their faces. It makes me feel needed and alive. I do enjoy the investigative, diagnostic dilemmas, which are approached like a detective but I am always looking for treatable illnesses and feel terribly empty when I discover a terminal illness. When patients come to my office, who can't hear, and I can irrigate their ears and remove the wax, it isn't romantic or intellectually stimulating, but they say, "wow, thanks doc, I can hear." It doesn't get any better for me then that. Treatable upper respiratory infections are exciting. Lacerations can be repaired and lumps and bumps can be removed. Diabetes, heart failure, and asthma can be controlled. But the best feeling is having a patient with breathing difficulties leave my office taking a deep unobstructed breath. These are my rewards from God. I spend a lot of time trying to prevent diseases, which is better than treatment. It is easier to prevent a stroke then treat a stroke. It is better to prevent a heart attack then to treat a heart attack. It is very difficult to encourage patients to change their life styles, and at times they get angry with me for what they view as my badgering them, but it's my job and I'm going to do it. The results are healthier, longer, more productive, enjoyable lives. Many of my patients in our farming community are very rugged, independent, self-starters and feel that they can live life without regard to health issues. When I talk to them about preventive medicine to control their blood pressure, their smoking, their weight, their cholesterol, their sugar, their activity or their life style, they say, "Well doc, it's OK If I die." I tell them that they are not going to die but that they will suffer for many years. They will walk around the supermarket with a tank of oxygen, or drag their leg with their hand strapped to their side while drooling out of the side of their mouth, or be forced to ride in a Wal-Mart motor cart because of arthritis made worse by obesity. I hope that this tactic eventually helps some of them to see the light, but without some outside motivation it may only occur when it is too late. My patients don't like this kind of talk, but isn't it my job to share the knowledge given to me? No one can do this by himself. Is this any different with our salvation? We don't like to be told that we have fallen short and are sinners and we must repent. No one likes to be told about their shortcomings even if they already know about them. In fact, maybe they become angrier, because they already know about their inadequacies. However, it is impossible to change if we don't acknowledge our need to change. As a doctor, I feel that it is easier for me personally to take my own advice because I see the end results of my patients indiscretions on a daily basis. I see the strokes and heart attacks and the chronic obstructive pulmonary disease from smoking. I get a booster shot of reality every day. I know the right solution and it is sad when patients fail to see the light. God is light and it is likewise sad, when people refuse His light, and the only spiritual cure for our separation from our Creator God. Jesus is the way and the truth and the life. What will it take for you to see and accept His counsel? The problem with my medical analogy is that the end result of unbelief cannot be reversed, because after death comes judgment. One of my diabetic patients came in my office to check her fasting blood sugar and it was very good in the therapeutic range. I told her that she was doing great and she said that Christmas was hard. It is hard to stay on a diabetic diet during Christmas but even harder to maintain that diet for every Christmas. We have all lost a ton of weight but we regain the weight again. We have to be committed to these goals forever. Forever is a long time and we need help from above. Maybe these words will help you, because they are true. There is an old expression, "Act in haste, repent in leisure." I encourage you; I beseech you, to take the cure, both physically and spiritually. Then, instead of repenting in leisure, you can rest and relax for eternity.

Patients are always showing me their new health formulas or magic elixirs. They ask me what they should do to be healthy. The answers are very simple and if patients are honest with themselves, they already know the proper solution. We need to be physically active which can be accomplished with a daily walking program. Smoking may be the greatest risk factor to health besides riding intoxicated on a motorcycle without a helmet. Alcohol should be consumed in moderation and we must eat the right quantity and types of food, resulting in a non-overweight body type. This last bit of advice seems to be the hardest for Americans. We work very hard at a desk job and return home to watch television or move a mouse on a computer while eating fast foods filled with carbohydrates and dripping with fat. If we exercise at all, we think that will make us lose weight and enable us to eat more. There is only one way to lose weight and when I tell my patients especially women, they dislike my advice and get angry with me. The only way to lose weight is to be hungry. That's against all the commercial advertisements that you have ever heard. When I tell my patients that they have to eat less, they all say, "But doc, I don't eat a lot now. Let me tell you what I just ate for breakfast." Weight loss is a function of eating less calories then you excrete. Exercise is required to tone muscles and keep your cardiovascular system free of plaque and develop a good recovery time, but to lose weight you have to exercise much more than we are willing to do or have the time to accomplish. Consider jogging five miles everyday and losing one hundred calories per mile. That's only a five hundred-calorie piece of pie, and very few people are willing or able to jog five miles on a daily basis. To lose weight, you must eat less.

When I go on the medical missionary trips to underprivileged nations, where food is scarce, no one is obese. The peoples of Tanzania or Kenya or China or Haiti are all very thin. When I go to these countries for a two-week period, I usually lose at least ten pounds. I'm not suggesting a starvation diet, but these trips demonstrate that our obesity problems are related to overeating due to our over-abundance and availability of delicious varied foods. It is also very interesting that different countries have different diseases based on body types and obvious genetic differences. The Indian peoples of India or Fiji and the people of Romania are hypertensive and have a high incidence of diabetes. The Chinese populous, seem to have a higher incidence of gastritis and allergies and asthma. The African community has a higher incidence of infections. Future epidemiological studies will help us to determine etiologies of these diseases, but at least it seems that obesity is directly related to diabetes, heart attacks, strokes and arthritis. More distressing to me is that obesity for the most part is preventable. The body is the temple of God and we have an obligation to care for this amazing temple that can sustain adversity and abuse and even repair itself. There is, however, a limit and we need not to go beyond that frontier. We need to be good stewards of our resources, our time and our bodies.

It is a tremendous joy for me to use my time and spiritual gifts in the service of God's people and the organization of "His Healing Hands" has given me an avenue to exercise these gifts. Who is the giver and who is the receiver? Who is getting the gift? .

After our return from China, Jeff and I have gotten our families involved in these missions and our families; especially Jeff's have become the leaders of "His Healing Hands." Carol, Jeff's wife has gone on many of these trips as a nurse and is the treasurer of the organization. Jeff's father and mother have also been on several missions and are directors of the organization, and Jeff's brother and sister-in-law are also participants and leaders. Jeff has become the president of "His Healing Hands." My three children and Jeff's two children have gone on many trips and are an integral part of these missions and they have been deeply affected by their experiences. They have made decisions concerning their futures based on prospective involvements in missionary work. These young people have added a vibrant element to our trips and opened up an avenue for other parents and their young children to join us. Last Christmas, my family spent our vacation, not in Disneyland or Hawaii, but in the garbage dump of Belize City. It was the best Christmas of our lives in many ways.

Christmas in a
City Dump

Christmas in the United States is a wonderful time of the year and our family has always looked forward to this festive holiday. With my son Paul, my brother-in-law, his wife and two children, we decided to spend Christmas in Belize on a medical missionary trip, partnering with Mission to the World. This was a big decision because Christmas at our home has always been a very strong American family tradition. My wife and my other son and daughter remained at home and I knew that they would greatly miss this Christmas family custom. Christmas in Belize sounds like a very avant-garde, secular, nouveau, American vacation. This would be true in a non-believing family, who traveled to Belize for a vacation of snorkeling, swimming, sun bathing and butterfly viewing. However, in a missionary minded Christian family, it means spending our time in the Belize City trash dump doing medical missionary work.

The various denominational churches in Belize wanted to form a church in the poor area of Belize City. The only land that was made available to them, at a very over inflated price, was a lot in the middle of the city trash dump. The city didn't think the group of churches would accept this horrible location. They agreed to the offer and started to build a church in the middle of the poorest area of the city. The congregations of these churches started to donate to this project and they had succeeded in completing the concrete foundation. They wanted to draw the poor people to the future church site and asked "His Healing Hands" to conduct a medical clinic on the exposed concrete foundation of this future church. We had helped them set up a medical clinic five years before on the northern portion of Belize and now it was a highly attended clinic and they didn't need us to go there again. We were now given the opportunity to draw the people to this dumpsite and help turn it into a church that would fulfill the needs of these people. God always goes where the needy people reside and He knows that the flowers always grow best over the garbage dump. God is the God of everyone. The Hebrew phrase in the Bible is that "God is not a respecter of persons."

My son, my brother-in-law and his family, with our missionary hosts in Belize City.

That means that God is never prejudicial and is always impartial. Rich or poor, brilliant or average, handsome or homely, short or tall; He gives everyone the opportunity to come to Him.

We held a medical clinic on the foundation of that future church and these poor, needy people were cared for and served. These people loved this concern for their welfare, and they were delighted to find out that a church was going to be built on that sight. Its hard to visualize the conditions in that city dump that "serves" as living quarters for any community, but it's all they had and it was home to them. The garbage in this dump represents the discarded, worthless, and useless stuff of the community, but these inhabitants were worthwhile and useful and shouldn't be discarded by us.

After our daily clinics, we walked around that city refuse dump where the people had built their homes in the hovel of that site. All their possessions and decorations were the discarded items of the people of Belize City. They were short on belongings but long on love. God is love and we tried to exhibit God's love to them. All peoples know how to respond to love. The children playing in the alleyways between the garbage piles occupy themselves in the same way as any children. These children laughed with joy and excitement during their made up games. This section of the city at first appeared depressive to us and we were dismayed, but these people were not "down in the dumps." This was evident by their family relationships and activity. We were the ones that were disheartened, seeing their living conditions. We were identifying and thinking that we would be unhappy in these surroundings. These people were doing the best they could under the circumstances and their joy and love surfaced and couldn't be held down. As usual, we learned a lot from these "unfortunate" people, or maybe we were the unfortunate ones, who don't appreciate our own lives. Life is not about possessions. It is about being possessed and overcome by the love of God.

The people of these poor countries that we try to help with our medical care and message of hope always remind me of growing up on the lower Eastside of New York City. I identify with them and I realize that "there but for the grace of God go I." Most big cities, even in the United States have their poor section of town, which contain needy, hopeless people. When I grew up in New York, my family was poor but I never knew it. As a kid, I had a lot of fun like all children but I was never hungry and I had unlimited opportunity in our free country. These children in Belize were no different than children in the United States. Children are children and people are people with the same needs, desires, and aspirations. All they need is a little help, opportunity and hope in the future. I have been participating in medical missionary work for the past six years and at first, I thought the medical care was why I was going to underprivileged areas. It is very important, but I have come to realize that hope is even more critical to the well being of all people, even more than medical care. The people of Belize are a combination of the ethnic groups: Blacks, Hispanics, Whites, and Caribbean. I mention this because I am very comfortable and at ease with these different groups, having grown up on the streets of New York. I love this mixture of ethnicity, especially when there is unity in this diversity. That's called being an American.

I loved my Jewish traditions and my Italian, Chinese, Puerto Rican, Black, and Irish friends with their different traditions. We were unified by our exuberant youth. The inner city of Belize is very similar to New York where I grew up in the fifties and sixties. It seems to me that there were a lot less rules and regulations during that period of time. We played stickball on the streets. We played cards sitting on egg crates and pitched pennies on the sidewalk. We gambled in the bowling alley and in the pool halls. We bought greasy, delicious hot dogs from the street vendors, and Italian scrapped ice cups from the pushcarts. When we got hurt, we just went over to the local hospital emergency room and they patched us up. As a youth, my goal was to become part of the Mafia of my friend's parents and I would have made it, except I wasn't Italian and therefore I would never be fully trusted. This appears to be a strange goal but to a young person on the streets, comradeship and belonging to an accepting group was everything. When I was fourteen years old, I spent a lot of time in the local bowling alley and I became a very good bowler. In fact, I was considering a professional bowling career. There were a group of my Asian and Italian friends who were gamblers and I became a type of mascot to them. I became the best bowler of the group and at the age of fifteen, my older companions took me all over the city to challenge and bet on my abilities. They were in their late teens and their early twenties, and we drove to different neighborhoods to confront and challenge their best bowlers. During these evenings of bowling, there was a lot of money changing hands and we usually won. I didn't bet on myself, as I didn't have any money, but they gave me part of the winnings and I would return home with fifty to seventy dollars in my pocket. This was a lot of money and sometimes more than my mother earned in a week. After an evening of gambling and driving around the city, we would end up in a Chinese or Italian restaurant of one of my friend's parents. It was after hours and they would open up the restaurant just for us. I never ordered anything but the most delicious homemade Chinese or Italian food just kept coming. I drove my mother crazy, as she would be hanging out our apartment window at three in the morning looking for her teenage son. My father had died when I was eight years old and these friends and their parents became my heroes and I felt accepted and important in the company of male companionship. Of course, at times I got into trouble and even spent a night in a holding cell of the local police station, but it always seemed that someone was looking after me. That specific evening, it was my mother that got me out of trouble.

One of my friends had just been "dumped" by his girlfriend and he was very upset. We were walking on Tenth Street and avenue B on a very hot and humid night with a lot of people sitting outside in front of storefront windows who were talking and playing cards. My friend in his anger and frustration over his girlfriend, picked up a chair and threw it into a storefront window. We started to run but a patrolling police car was called and caught up with us. My friend told me not to "rat" on him as he had been in jail several times and the police were looking to throw the book at him. Years later, he was sent to prison for murder and died in prison. I had never been in any type of trouble and he told me not to implicate him. We were taken to the police station and separated. The police told me that my friend said that I had thrown the chair. With a clear conscious I denied it. Then they asked me, if my friend had done it, but I didn't want to lie. I told them, I didn't do it. Again, they asked if he had done it and I said, "I didn't do it." I kept answering the question in this manner. They were trying to frighten me with threats and I blurted out in a bold statement that I didn't care as long as they didn't call my mother. They immediately got her on the phone. I don't know exactly what she said to them but after telling her that I was in jail, they were never able to get another word into the conversation. Later, I found out that she kept telling them that I was a good boy and got good grades in school and never had ever got into trouble. These officers who were trying to badger me were badgered by my mother. They would rather let me go then talk to her and they immediately sent me on my way. My Jewish mother had saved me from prison.

When I look at the children playing in the city dump of Belize City, I see myself and the friends of my youth. What chance do they have without God? What chance did I have without God? I can vividly remember lying in my bed at night after my father had died and thinking that there was no one to take care of me. At the same time, I knew that my Jewish God of Abraham, Isaac, and Jacob was watching over me. It was just a feeling at that time but I later found out that it was true and God was waiting for me to knock on the door and have a personal relationship with Him. God is available to all of us, but He has given us free will and He won't invade our lives unless we ask voluntarily and with an opened heart and mind.

Christmas in Belize was the real holiday, because Christmas is about giving and not receiving. It is about God humbling Himself to stoop so low as to take on human form as our kinsman redeemer to lead a sinless life, die as a substitute for us and rise again, so we can eventually follow Him for eternity. Simply stated; He came forth from the Father into the world, to pay the price for us all, and go back to the Father. Christmas is Jesus' gift to us and what better way to spend Christmas than to share His gift with others. When we left for Belize at Christmas, we felt that we would be giving up our holiday but we arrived back home gaining a "Holy Day."

Some of these medical missionary trips appear dangerous to our relatives and friends praying for us back home. I don't feel that these expeditions are at all risky, but that may be because I know that God is with us and watching over us. God's protection and care was evident on our medical missionary trip to Kenya. This trip to Kenya was planned with excitement and anticipation and I was looking forward to that trip especially because my son Paul was joining our team on the journey. Looking back on that adventure, we really were in danger and at risk.

Masai woman in Kenya applies cow dung to make the walls of her home.

Dodge City of the Old West in Kenya

Before we left for Nairobi, Kenya, there was an article in the Los Angeles Times concerning the "worst" ghetto in Africa and probably the worst in the world called "Deep Sea." This hovel contains fifteen hundred people on four acres with only one faucet with polluted water and no toilets. They defecate into plastic bags, knot the opening and throw them on their tin roofs. When the wind blows these bags soar all around the compound, and they call them flying toilets. Their "homes" are made of red mud between sticks, covered by thin tin roofs. At night there are roving gangs demanding protection money. Across a polluted river is a wealthy community by African standards. Most of these people in this ghetto are newly arrived immigrants coming from the desert looking for a better quality of life. This sub-Saharan African ghetto had the highest incidence of infectious diseases on the planet. After reading about that horrible place, I said, "Lord, I hope we're not going there." I didn't know it at the time, but that was exactly where we were to hold our first few clinic days. God uses us wherever He sees fit based on the area of the greatest need for His witness and the most urgent concern for His people. We arrived in Nairobi, Kenya via New York, and London. Africa is always exciting but the poverty and squalor is juxtaposed next to modern city buildings which makes for a stark contrast. We stayed in a very basic Christian missionary hotel where we met many other American Christian missionaries. They were mostly social service type of people and when they found out that we were medical personnel, they told us of their medical needs and we held a mini-medical clinic for them. This scenario has occurred repeatedly in hotels where we stay, as everyone has medical requests and it turns out to be a great Christian witness. We meet a lot of wonderful humanitarian people and it is amazing how many of them are Americans. I am astounded at the giving nature of the citizens of our country. The world may criticize the strongest country in the world but they truly need and appreciate us when we support and minister to them. When we arrived in the "Deep Sea" ghetto we saw the identical scene that was photographed in the news article. I laughed at God's sense of humor

Deep Sea Ghetto in Nairobi, Kenya

and my naïve approach. Actually, the scene was worse because we could smell it, hear it, feel the heat, and we had to avoid and duck out of the way of the flying toilets. How could man let other men live like this? Even though, we are a small group, we tried to improve their conditions in a modest way. We set up our clinic and worked from dawn to dusk and treated four hundred citizens of that ghetto on a daily basis. We couldn't stay after dark, as it was too dangerous. It is easy to start a clinic in the morning but very difficult to end it at night, as there is always another person who wants to be seen when we have to leave. We had a group of very helpful young people with us and this experience has affected their approach to life since those days in that African ghetto. They say Africa changes a man inside and that he will never be the same. It's true. Africa is immense and its physical conditions can be very harsh, but the cruelty of Africa lies within its uncompromising tribal feuds, its brutal governments, its abject poverty, and its unyielding diseases made worse by cultural practices. From my perspective, it is impossible to change Africa and there seems to be nowhere to start. But I can help one person at a time and I can improve the health and hideous conditions of that person for at least a short period of his life. I feel called by God to do what I can through His healing hands.

We thought that we had seen the most severe conditions but we underestimated the unkindness of the Sahara desert. After treating the majority of the patients of the "Deep Sea," we headed to the town of Osiolo on the way to the very remote village of Merti in the Sahara desert on the road to Ethiopia and the Sudan. We headed to the middle of nowhere, a destination not on anyone's map. In speaking to the desk clerk in our Nairobi hotel, he was very surprised when we told him that we were going to Merti. He said that he had never heard of any foreigners going to Osiolo and that he had never heard of Merti. We had a lot of trouble rounding up enough four-wheel drive vehicles to take into the desert. When they did arrive, I noticed that they didn't have spare tires.

We traveled north from Nairobi and eventually this "all weather road" ended and we were traveling in the sand of the desert. There weren't any tracts and our driver was going north by dead reckoning into the wilderness leaving any sign of civilization behind, however, there didn't seem to be any indication of civilization in front of us. The only sign, we saw was a plaque designating the crossing of the equator through an African village. There was a man squatting down with a pitcher of water, a funnel and a bowl. We stopped and he told us that water would run in different circles on either side of the equator. I didn't believe this myth. He was right and it wasn't an old wives' tale. On one side of the equator it ran clockwise and when he stepped over to the other side of the equator it ran counter-clockwise. Maybe it was a trick but it looked real. We gave him some coins and continued on our

Osiolo, Kenya, the last outpost before entering the
Sahara Desert from the South.
It was like Dodge City of the Old West

journey to Osiolo. The sand in front of us was endless and barren, doted by a few stick huts with grass roofs along the way. Even these huts disappeared but once in awhile we would see a nomadic goat herder in the sparse bushes seemingly coming from nowhere and headed nowhere. Trucks loaded with bags of some type of supplies and crowded with humanity sitting on the top of these supplies and hanging onto the sides of the vehicle came from the opposite direction. After several hours we arrived in the town of Osiolo. We were told by our hosts that we needed to stock up on food, water and gasoline in Osiolo because it was the last settlement before the heart of the desert and the wilderness. We thought that we were already in the wilderness.

Osiolo was like Dodge City in the old American Wild West. It was an untamed outpost with people everywhere, bartering all types of goods and "services." We got out of our vehicles in the center of town in front of a general store and made sure that the women of our group were always accompanied by some of the males. The store had bottled water, one jar of peanut butter, cookies and sacks of rice. We bought all the water and rice that we could carry plus boxes of cookies and that one jar of peanut butter. We had not been told that there wasn't any food in Merti until we arrived in Osiolo and we were not adequately prepared. We gassed up in the only petrol station in town and started to head out of this settlement. I asked our driver if we had enough gasoline for the return trip and he said that he wasn't sure. We stopped our caravan of ten, four-wheel drive vehicles, rounded up "jerry" cans and filled them with extra gasoline for the return trip, as there was no gas available in Merti. I was starting to be concerned. What if we got a flat tire, ran out of water and food, or ran out of gas? We stopped again to do what we should have done all along, we prayed. My faith had been increasing as I went on more of these missionary trips but this was a true test of my reliance on God.

As a youth, I grew up learning to rely on myself in New York City, which helped me survive in the "concrete jungle," but now I was learning to rely on God and not on my own scheming, calculating, and manipulative ways. This relying on someone other than myself gave me a very unsteady, unstable, and unbalanced feeling. I was vulnerable but my faith in God was much stronger than my faith in myself. I realized this was beyond my control and I started to take pleasure in leaning on God instead of relying on myself. I felt that we were in the will of God and this missionary endeavor was His plan and therefore, it was His responsibility to protect us. I knew that He was infinitely more capable than me. I was at the mercy of the desert but He created the desert. God is always in complete control and all we had to do was be filled with His Holy Spirit doing His will. It was His deal, not mine. I actually began to enjoy the atmosphere of Osiolo, and I was excited about our adventure into the Sahara Desert and the remote village of Merti. Faith in God creates the proper attitude for service and love for others. We can't serve others or love them if we are concerned and worried about ourselves. Fear can be protective, if we can get away from the source of dread. However, fear can be paralyzing, creating a feeling of helplessness; resulting in an inability to act. In my experience, the terror that is generated in me is usually a waste of time.

When Jesus was asked about the most important commandment, He said, "To love God with all your heart, and mind and soul and to love each other as yourself." We call this the "Golden Rule." The Bible says that God is love, and we can reflect this love by loving each other. It has always seemed easier to me, to love God and more difficult to love His creation. This really doesn't make sense as I am one of His creations and He loves me and yet I am a sinner like everyone else. The only way that we can know ourselves is to know God, who created us, giving

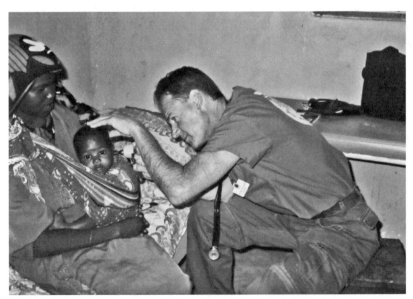

Examining a young patient in the desert village of Merti

Goat, our dinner was being prepared, organs included.

us some of His attributes. We must look to the original and not the copies. In our culture, we have heroes that we emulate, like rock stars and famous movie personalities. Why not make the Creator and our Savior our hero? There is a story about the Internal Revenue Service trying to recognize counterfeit bills by studying these bills. They spent a lot of time with these counterfeit bills under the microscope of their scrutiny. This didn't improve their ability to recognize these bills until someone suggested that they were going about it the wrong way. The new suggestion was to study the original and know all it's details and then they would be able to recognize the frauds. This worked and their recognition of the counterfeit improved. We must do the same thing. We must study the architect, the designer, the original, our maker and then we will know God and know ourselves. The Book of Jeremiah says that we should not boast in our wisdom or our strength or our riches but we can boast in our knowledge and understanding of God. How can I claim to know God or myself, if I don't love my fellow man? This too was about to be tested in Merti.

The road to Merti started out as a potholed asphalt highway but disappeared into a desert sand road without any discernible tracts. Our driver assured me that he knew the way. However, he stopped many times to consult with the other drivers and to make sure we stayed in a caravan with visual contact between all of the vehicles. Even though we were on a desert road, we traveled at least fifty miles per hour and we bottomed out repeatedly. I prayed that we wouldn't break a hole in the gas tank as we hit boulders buried in the sand. It reminded me of an unfinished road I took in 1970 from Las Vegas to Los Angeles.

I was motoring across the country from New York City after graduating from medical school in June with the goal of starting my internship in Los Angeles in July. I loved driving across the country, leaving the big city and traveling through the heartland of our great country. I had lived in the shadows of skyscrapers all my life but had never seen the steel mills of Pittsburgh. I had eaten meat all my life but I had never seen beef cattle in the stockyards of Sioux City, Iowa. I had eaten cereals, and corn and grains but I had never traveled through the

Camels at an oasis in the middle of the Sahara Desert.

miles of wheat, corn and grain fields. I had read about the Lewis and Clark Expedition but had never seen the Mississippi or Missouri Rivers. The Badlands, Mount Rushmore, Yosemite Valley, and the Grand Canyon were awesome. In 1970, route 15 from Las Vegas to Los Angeles was just being completed, but even though it had a temporary barrier, I was told it was drivable. I went around the barriers in order to save at least two hours of travel time. I took the road by myself into the Mohave Desert in the summer on an unfinished road traveling sixty-five miles per hour. I gripped the wheel and my knuckles were white during the entire uncertain trip. Parts of the highway were incomplete and it was illegal and foolhardy to travel on an unfinished road at high speeds. On the road to Merti, I remembered that anxious feeling of never knowing what was around the bend of that desert road. After three hours of true off-roading and catching air, we stopped at a desert oasis, complete with herds of camels, sheep and goats protected by nomadic shepherds. We tried to take their pictures but they picked up stones to threaten us. We wondered if our arrival in Merti would have the same reaction. We headed into the deserted sand and two hours

Village of Merti with thatched roofs over mud huts

later, we saw a few hills with a village of huts in the distance under the shadow of small knolls.

When we arrived in Merti, the people who had been told that we were coming started to appear out of their stick and mud huts. They lined the main avenue to cheer, clap, and just gawk, at the American medical missionaries. It was like a motorcade or ticket tap parade. We had never experienced anything like this and we waved excitedly back to these expectant people. We drove up a small hill to find a type of monastery with the Catholic Priest awaiting us. He couldn't be more excited to see us. He was an Italian Priest named, Gicovi, and he hadn't had any visitors for over eight months. He was literally jumping up and down with the biggest smile that I had ever seen. We were overjoyed at this reception, until we realized that one of our vehicles with our host's infant daughter was missing.

The head of Campus Crusade for Christ had arranged for us to go to Merti, and he took his wife and infant, nursing baby in the caravan with us but not in the same vehicle that he drove. He had to lead the convoy, as he was the only person that had been in Merti before our trip. When we disembarked, the truck with the baby was not with us. His wife had also been in a separate automobile. We were all aghast and we gathered together and prayed for the safety of this baby. We had to unload our supplies, our food and medicines and equipment, and arrange for our sleeping quarters, which were bunk beds without sheets on earthen floors with few toilet facilities. We were very busy but a pall of dread and concern was hanging over us. As a father, identifying with the parents, and having my own son with me, I was uneasy, tense, anxious, and panicky. The apprehension was overwhelming for me, and yet this godly father was going about the compound helping all of us get settled in. He then left to back track into the desert to find his infant daughter after trying to console his wife. We all had to organize and make a lot of arrangements and greet many people but my heart and thoughts were with those distressed parents. Every time one of our group passed another member of the team, they stopped to pray. The sun went down but the father hadn't returned. We ate a dinner of rice with bits of goat and goat gravy flavoring but it stuck in my throat. Finally after several hours, the father returned without the child. We prayed most of the night but had to sleep to get some rest for the morning clinic. Our accommodations were pretty bare and primitive but our thoughts were occupied with the child and the distraught parents. The desert is unforgiving and treacherous and I knew that a nursing child without his mother had little chance. How would the people in the other transport feed the baby? Would they run out of gas, lost in the cold desert at night? Would they be safe? Their survival was truly in God's hand. Maybe it was the thought of a dependent child or the anguish of the parents that made me think of our vulnerability and complete need to rely on God. But aren't we all vulnerable and completely dependent on God for our survival at all times? If we don't have the Lord in all, we don't have the Lord at all. Our coronary arteries are pencil thin. Our vessels to our brain are even smaller, and our heart must

Colorfully dressed ladies of a certain tribe in Merta, Kenya

beat seventy times per minute for over seventy years without stopping to rest. We are dynamic organisms in a constant state of flux between coagulation and anti-coagulation, between taking in nutrients and detoxifying and excreting poisons, and between oxygenating our cells and deoxygenating them. Who controls all this? The answer is obviously not man. As the dawn approached and the sun came up, the father again left to search the desert for his child. We ate a meager breakfast and prepared for our first clinic day in the desert town of Merti.

Walking with our medical supplies to our clinic site, we saw the jubilant father and mother clutching their lost child. It was impossible that the lost child was alive and well after spending the night in a truck in the middle of the Sahara Desert. There is no question in my mind that God, in a miraculous way, protected and returned this child to her godly parents. The people of Merti probably thought that these Americans were crazy as we literally were jumping for joy and hugging each other in the middle of the dusty road. What a clinic we had. We couldn't stop laughing and hugging and smiling. After a few hours, our host arrived in the clinic clutching his baby whom he wouldn't let go for a second. God had blessed all of us beyond belief. This trial and mental tribulation created by our own human poor judgment was turned around and used by God to increase our reliance on Him and expand our faith and our belief in His providential loving care. God is not the author of these trials but He allows them to occur and changes their effect from a negative influence to a positive persuasion and evidence of His great love for His children. Again, God upheld both sides of the equation to increase my faith. Besides God's direct influence on me, the parents were an example to me of deep Christian faith in God.

They had never given up hope or the belief that God would provide the way of escape from this predicament. They searched for their child and continued in prayer. They traveled through the immense barren desert and never gave up on God's fertile promises. They never wavered because they put themselves in God's unwavering hands. They were an example to me and the rest of the team. God never presents us with more than we can handle, but very honestly, I don't think that I have enough faith as yet to handle this type of scenario. These parents made me think of Abraham who was willing to place his son in God's hands. This was a foretelling of God allowing and sending His own Son as a sacrifice to suffer and die for our sins. Can you imagine having that kind of trust, hope and faith in God? We do have a God of love and we are able to love God and each other because He loved us first,

Two of our cars had broken windows as a result of "stoning" after we showed the Jesus Film to the Islamic village of Merti

even when we were yet sinners. If we love God, we must love all those that are created in His image. After this child was found, her parents couldn't stop hugging and clinging to her. I couldn't stop hugging my son and thanking the Son. Our physical conditions and accommodations in this monastery setting were not optimal to say the least but we didn't mind. We were focusing on God and not ourselves and we fell in love with the people of Merti.

These people were in the middle of a draught and were starving. When we ate our meals, they came to our camp to share our food. It is impossible to eat while others who are starving are watching you. Of course, we invited all of them to share our food and over the period of one week, we ran out of food. In ten days in Kenya, I lost ten pounds. I needed to lose weight but I don't advise others to do it as we did in Kenya. The people were very grateful for our medical care but we were in for a big surprise.

We had a team with us from Campus Crusade for Christ and they asked the local Sheik if they could show the Jesus film to his people. He hesitated but due to his gratefulness for our care of his people, he acquiesced to the showing of the film that evening. These nomadic, Islamic people were enthralled with the film shown in the middle of their village, however, at the end of the film, the mothers told their children to pick up stones and stone us. They broke two of our car windows and hit one of our helpers. No one was seriously injured but this was a very threatening experience and we needed to travel six hours in those vehicles through the desert on our return home. We were a bit shaken but we needed to continue to show God's love. We discussed among ourselves whether or not we should hold a clinic in the morning. We all know the New Testament "notion" of turning the other cheek but this was literally our cheek and it was time to put our money where our mouth was and trust and obey God without animosity to our fellow man. The next day we held our medical clinic and everybody in the village showed up as if to test us. We treated all the patients, even the ones that had thrown stones. As a New York street person, I had never reacted to an assault in this way. In my youth in the city, if you didn't retaliate and respond with aggression to an attack, you were liable to be mistreated and abused again. We all have to learn and sometimes it takes a concrete test. I guess we passed the test because the people were even friendlier than before and they expressed their gratitude to all of us. That evening we had a farewell dinner and the village people killed a goat in our honor. We feasted on rice and all parts of the prized goat without leaving out any goat organs. I must admit that I only ate the rice and my last few cookies that I had bought in Osiolo. The priest, Father Gicovi Michael, was delighted with our visit and begged us to return to Merti in the future. He has been e-mailing us for the past year,

Packed church in Merti, Kenya

begging us to return and we are planning a return trip in the spring. We left Merti at four in the morning to avoid traveling in the hot desert with two of our car windows taped and hoping that our gas and tires would last for the entire journey back to Nairobi. We had seen a part of Africa that is rarely seen by tourists but is a true picture of the difficult, sometimes cruel realistic conditions of the African Desert. In the last hour of our six-hour trip with our ten vehicles, one of the cars got a flat tire just at the outskirts of Osiolo. God protected us for twelve hours in the hot desert without a breakdown and without potential disasters. We were able to replace the tire in Osiolo and return safely to civilization in Nairobi. Africa changes a man's perspective with regard to the environment, to life and self- worth, and to your relationship to God and to others. None of us returned home unchanged, and we were all eager to go on our next missionary trip after a little rest and relaxation. This brings up an interesting point. In spite of difficult conditions in the field, we get to leave and return to our plush lives. No matter how difficult these conditions are for us, we know what is waiting for us at home. The people of Merti are home, and remain there forever without the hope of a better life. Maybe, we gave them some comfort and eased their life for a short period of time.

We were learning from our experiences and we were beginning to feel confident that we were able to handle these medical missionary trips with aplomb and self-assuredness, until the forces of "Nature" intervened. Tsunamis, hurricanes and earthquakes changed our well-laid plans and shook us out of our secure complacency. We were about to be forced into a more acute medical responding organization.

It is Better to be Given the Tools to Fish - Than to be Given Fish

When the Tsunami struck South East Asia it was estimated that over two hundred thousand people died in the "natural" disaster and many more people were made homeless and instantly became impoverished. "His Healing Hands" was called to respond. Our families had gotten used to our going to remote places but Indonesia was very anti- American, anti –Christian, and pro- Islamic fundamentalist. Bandi Ach was controlled by radical Islamic terrorists. God was going to widen our horizons again in going to areas where we aren't wanted by the majority of the population. Did Jesus come for the righteous or did He come to serve sinners? Are Christians called only to serve believers or are we called to seek the "lost?" Should we only serve in areas where we are comfortable or should we provide care where God calls us? Many Christian organizations are not allowed to go to Islamic countries but as a medical humanitarian organization we were being asked to help in areas where the Gospel has never been allowed. We look upon our medical service only as a tool to show the love of our Creator God to the world. Since this is our prime mission, we couldn't deny this calling or this opportunity.

Our directors met to discuss the vision and the purpose of our medical missionary organization and whether we could expand our mission to include disaster relief. We understood that we were not first responders, because that was mostly the purview of governmental organizations who can supply helicopters, naval task forces, bulldozers and an armed forces organization, backed by the monetary power of governments, mostly the United States. When a catastrophe strikes, the media surrounds the disaster site, followed by army relief. After two to three weeks, the media and world opinion cools and the refugees need medical care, water, warm clothes, and tents. There is a void that forms and "His Healing Hands" could definitely fill that void, as we have now shown in Indonesia, Mississippi, and Pakistan.

When the United States offered aid in the form of the United States Navy, the government of Indonesia begrudgingly accepted the offer with a specific deadline and extraction date for the troops to leave their country. This date of departure was arranged even before they arrived. They made it known that they didn't want Americans helping them but they knew they had no choice, as we were the only country with the resources to help their people. After several months of search and rescue and clean up, the populous needed medical supplies, medical personnel and fishing boats. "His Healing Hands" with the help of Campus Crusade for Christ and Global Aid Network International arranged to supply these needs to the Island of Nias, on the west coast of Indonesia, which was in the direct path of the Tsunami. Jeff Walker the president of "His Healing Hands," called me to co-lead a medical relief team to Indonesia. My first reaction was "Here we go again." I keep telling myself that faith and sanctification are processes and they are ongoing developments. This makes perfect sense, as sanctification is a process whereby we are becoming more like Jesus on a daily basis, reflecting His glory, and faith is developing confidence in God's control and providential care. Going on these trips have nothing to do with courage and everything to do with reliance on God. All these trips were opportunities to serve God and His created beings and we were being given the privilege and honor to represent Him as His ambassadors. I look back on my life and I realize that God has brought me a long way

Our Indonesian medical team

but the more I learn, the more I know that my path may be getting somewhat straighter but it seems to be longer. The more I learn, the more I need to learn. At the very least, my life will always be exciting and will never become boring or dull.

We were able to get visas for Indonesia and we formed a medical team consisting of several doctors including a doctor from Australia and myself, a pharmacist, Jeff, several nurses and other paramedical personnel. Victor from "Campus Crusade for Christ" had arranged for "Global Aid International Network" to partner with our organization. They had arranged to ship medical supplies from Germany to Indonesia and they had made a contact on the island of Nias, through the governor of the province. Our three organizations were able to get donations to have dugout canoes made to supply forty families with individual boats so they could return to their livelihood of fishing. In addition to getting these families to be self-sufficient again, it gave additional jobs to the local boat builders. Due to the horrific effects of the Tsunami, the fisherman were initially afraid to go back into the water but as time advanced, they needed to earn a living for their families in the only profession that they had ever known; fishing. I have lived in California for over thirty-six years and I have experienced four major earthquakes and several minor earthquakes and many aftershocks. The earth moves in a rolling direction or in waves across the room or lifts you up and down in staccato jerks. It is very unsettling. All our lives, we get accustomed to variation and change and instability but we expect the earth beneath our feet to stay put. When the earth moves and throws you to the ground, it is more than frightening; it is disquieting, disconcerting, and disturbing. You lose the confidence in something you always took for granted. The Tsunami for these boat people, who spent their entire life near and in the sea, was emotionally the most distressing event of their lives in addition to the obvious disaster of losing loved ones and all their material possessions including their homes. They needed help. We supplied them with boats, treated their ailments and gave them encouragement and hope.

They knew that we came in the love of God and understood that we believed in the God of the Bible. We will never know, what impact we had on these people but they accepted our love and returned the love, demonstrated by their smiles that had eluded their faces since the Tsunami had destroyed their lives. These islanders continue to ask us to return to their island and we have had three other teams return to Nias in the past six months.

After an exhaustive weekend of flying from Los Angeles to Tokyo to Singapore, we arrived in the City of Medan, Indonesia in the province of Sumatra. We were met by the governor of the district, who we accompanied, to the island of Nias in a military cargo plane. We boarded the plane from the belly of the plane and sat in seats made for paratroopers. As we flew to the island of Nias, we viewed the destruction, which was complete. Trees flattened, homes in piles of rubble, and the earth and terrain laid bare for at least five miles from the beach. These are similar scenes that are aired on the television of the world, but the

Fishing boats that were made in Nias, Indonesia, paid for by American donors.

view from the ground; seeing the people and caring for their needs is a view the media doesn't portray. The emotional and psychological effects of this disaster on the people can only be dealt with, by encouragement, love and hope that only God can give through His representatives. We touched down in Nias airport and were driven to a village on the beach where we had a ceremony to present the forty boats premade on the island to the families of the village that had been totally wiped out by the Tsunami. These people were delighted to get the "keys" to their new source of revenue to provide for their families. We prayed and dedicated their boats and asked God to protect and provide for their families. We held a small clinic on the beach and treated the people for their medical problems. This day was a perfect example of why I love our humanitarian medical missionary trips. They are adventuresome, exciting, and afford concrete, specific, direct help to needy people. It is wonderful for the world to donate money for disaster relief but these benefactors never see where the money goes and whether it is directly useful to its disadvantaged people. We provide direct medical care, specific staples of life; like food, clothing, tents and medicines, and we directly hand them to the people in need. What better thing could I ever do with my life and how much more joy could I ever experience in my life? These destitute people, after getting medical care for their entire families, rowed away in their new boats. Would they remember the Americans that came from the other side of the world to help them? Would they remember the God of the universe? Would they be grateful? There is no doubt that these disadvantaged people would remember each time they took their boat out and caught a fish and cooked that fish for their families or sold extra fish to support their family. This is the nature of humanitarian aid with people directly helping people just because it is the right thing to do since we are made in the image of a righteous God. There are many people who support our ministry with prayers and financial aid. These people don't go with us and see the effects of their assistance but they are a part of our humanitarian mission. There are many drug representatives that give me sample medicines to take on our trips and they also don't see these deprived people. I firmly believe that we will all meet in heaven, and some of these people will come up to other people who they have never physically met on earth and they will thank them for their care and concern. This love of friendship and sacrifice is what makes us human.

After dedicating these boats, we traveled to Ginung Sitoli, the capital city of Nias, where we stayed in the section of the local hospital that was still standing. This hospital was immense with many rooms made of unreinforced concrete that had collapsed on the patients. We stayed in a newer wing of the hospital, which we were told also collapsed one week after we left, due to an aftershock. I hadn't slept in this type of old hospital bed since I was an intern on call in the seventies, at U.C.L.A. There were hundreds of nurses in starched white uniforms complete with starched nurses hats, but these nurses didn't perform any medical functions. In fact they didn't know how to take a blood pressure of even put on a pair of gloves. We were told that the hospital administrator performed surgery when needed. I asked how the patients fared and he said they did fine, except for a lot of complications. We made the best of these deplorable conditions and we made rounds in the hospital and did what we could with our limited supplies. We performed some minor surgeries, like draining abscesses and repairing lacerations and gave out an assortment of antibiotics for infections. These ineffective, unprepared and unschooled medical personnel would be easy to criticize if we hadn't experienced these inadequacies in the beginnings of our own medical careers.

I remember my first month as an intern on the cardiology service in July of 1970 at Wadsworth Veterans Administration Hospital, which was affiliated, with U.C.L.A. The very first night that I was on call in the intensive care unit, one of the patients had a cardiac arrest. I stood over the bedside and an experienced nurse slipped defibrillation panels into my hands and told me to push the button. I did as I was told and the patient jumped. Nothing happened on the cardiac monitor and she told me to try again. This time after he jumped, the monitor showed a regular beat. The nurse said, "Good job doctor, you saved this man's life." I had just completed four years of medical school, passed my boards and knew a lot of medical theory, but this was reality and application. Knowledge without application is a futile exercise in self- indulgence, which is why internships and residencies are mandatory. I remember the feeling of complete inadequacy and how grateful I was for those experienced, battle tested, kind nurses. Maybe that's why I later married a nurse. After three months on the cardiac service, I was on my way to becoming a real doctor and not just a paper tiger.

On another occasion, one of my patients in the cardiac care unit developed a bradycardia, which means their pulse was too slow. This patient started to go into congestive heart failure with fluids backing up into his lungs, as his heart output couldn't keep up with the fluid input. With the help of my highly qualified nurses who had years of experience in the cardiac unit with both life threatening illnesses and unskilled, green, unproven interns like myself, we started on a course of action. This patient was rapidly getting symptomatic and we started oxygen, and gave him atropine intravenously to raise his pulse. This didn't work and he was sliding into severe congestive heart failure. We then gave him isoproterenol intravenously as an intravenous drip, which likewise yielded us no response. I called the resident to come into the hospital to put a temporary cardiac pacemaker into this rapidly deteriorating patient. He refused to come in and told me to temporize. This patient was dying before my eyes. The nurse offered to guide me through the procedures to place a ventricular pacemaker. I had never done this before or even watched it being done. I called the resident again and again he refused to come to the hospital. "We" decided to act. She guided me through the entire procedure and the poor alert patient was skeptical and scared, and so was I. Many times the catheter in the ventricle will not capture the beat to increase the heart rate, and the procedure has to be done several times. In this case we were fortunate and it captured the first pass of the catheter. The heart rate was set at seventy-two and the patients congestive heart failure was reversed. Those nurses were my best advisors and counselors and as a scared rookie intern, I couldn't be any more grateful to them.

The next day, I had to present my cases to the attending physician on medical rounds. I described the patient's symptomatic bradycardia and my treatment of atropine, and isoproterenol without results. I proceeded to tell him that "we" placed a pacemaker into the patient with capture and good resolution of the congestive heart failure. The resident, who refused to come to the hospital, dropped his stethoscope and his jaw. The attending physician looked at him and said, "good job" and we moved on to the next patient. I had learned many lessons. I learned to trust a patient's history, trust nurses and to rely on myself if I had the proper knowledge. I also learned to evaluate a situation presented to me by people under my care and to respond with integrity and responsibility without taking my personal comfort into account. I believe that resident also learned that lesson.

There was another situation that stands out in my memory but this involved my rookie intern when I was his resident. I had a very ill patient with kidney failure and nephrotic syndrome. I stayed by his bedside for many evenings monitoring him and treating him, but this night was my night off and I needed the rest. My intern was going to be in charge and he would have to "solo." He was very unsure of himself and I was unsure of his abilities. I had put a lot of time into this patient and we had developed a friendship and rapport. This inexperienced intern was going to be a real responsible doctor some day and I had to delegate responsibility to him and accept the consequences for my patient and me. I went home, left him in charge and hoped and prayed for the best. I returned to the ward the next day with trepidation, only to find my patient alive and better than when I left him the night before. Everyone needs a chance to come up to the bar.

The nicely dressed medical personnel in the hospital in Ginung Sitoli, Nias were untrained but they were very responsive to our treatment of the patients in the hospital and they soaked up everything we taught them. Afterward, they turned around to proudly show the other nurses what they had learned and to share their new knowledge with them. This goes right to the heart of the old medical expression of " See one, do one, teach one." After treating the patients in the hospital every morning, we packed up our medical supplies and went into the mountains and jungle of Nias to hold medical clinics in small remote villages, which never get medical care. We went to a different village every day and treated about two hundred patients per day.

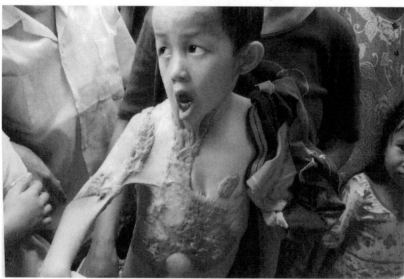

Polinius, a little boy, burned in a fire, who was later flown to the Philippines for multiple plastic surgeries.

In one of these villages we saw a little boy named Polinius, who had fallen into a fire several years ago with destructive results. He had miraculously healed his second and third degree burns but the debilitating scars were shocking and devastating. In the healing process, the scars had attached his chin to his right shoulder, freezing his chin in place to the right side and making his right shoulder, right arm and right elbow deformed, useless and functionless. His mother brought him to our clinic to see if there was any help for this delightful child. Obviously, there was nothing we could do at that moment but we took his name and said we would try to arrange something. We contacted our liaison in Global Aid International Network and they agreed to pay for his airfare to the United States, if we could arrange for his surgical care. This was going to take a lot of coordination, and a plastic surgeon, who would be willing to perform multiple reconstructive surgeries on this boy, in addition to housing the boy and his family for long periods of time.

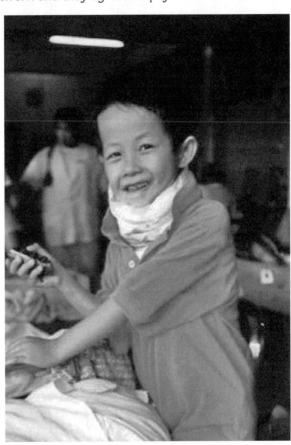

Polinius, after multiple plastic surgeries.

One month later, His Healing Hands sent a second team to Ginung Sitoli, Nias, and one of the team members was a physician from the Philippines. She was able to reconnect with the boy's family and arrange for his surgery in the Philippines. After multiple procedures, he was able to have a mobile neck with full range of motion, and the complete functional use of his shoulder, elbow and hand. A great deal of planning, effort, and arrangements went into the care of this little boy but his life was completely changed from being a lifelong invalid to being a useful citizen. What

Polinius, with the medical staff

is one life worth to society? What is one life worth to this little boy's father and mother, and to the boy himself? What is one soul worth to God? If God created all of us and He is Father to all of us, and we are His children, then one life is worth everything. This was a very dramatic story with sensational results, but all the people we treat have stories to tell. They may not be as thrilling and breathtaking but they are never the less very important. If we can alleviate some pain and suffering in some small way in the people that we contact, then I believe God is pleased with us and we are doing His biding. There is a story about a man walking along a beach at sunset, who came across a young boy bending down repeatedly, picking up starfish washed up on the beach from low tide, and throwing them back into the sea to save them. The man saw hundreds of starfish and he said to the young man, "You can't possibly save all these fish, along this beach, so how can you possibly make a difference?" The boy smiled, bent down, picked up another starfish and threw it back into the sea and said, "It made a difference to that one." Every life is of value to God and the world.

Everywhere we treated patients in Indonesia, the Islamic people knew that we were Christian missionaries and they received us and accepted our help. They didn't harass us or fight with us or argue with us. They were grateful and appreciative and I believe that we changed some minds and hearts and ideas. Love will break down all barriers and bridge all gaps, if it is genuine love from God. This trip to Indonesia after the Tsunami was our first journey involving post disaster relief. We were able to help appropriately and our team was so excited about the results that we have subsequently sent two more teams to Indonesia with more trips planned for the future. With this experience, we were able to accept and prepare for our next post disaster relief trip to Pakistan after their catastrophic

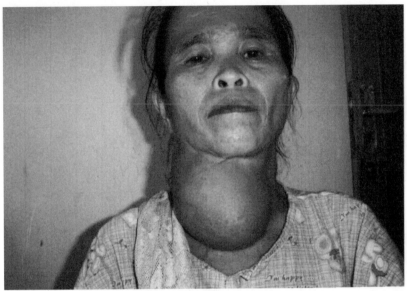

Typical patient with a Thyriod goiter, very common in Indonesia

7.9 earthquake in the rugged frigid Himalayan Mountains with winter and snow approaching. Although we had now been active in medical missionary work for several years and our families had gotten accustomed to our traveling to many strange and at times unknown destinations, The Republic of Pakistan was a frightening concept to our apprehensive families.

Some of our team members with the village chiefs in the
Ghari Habibullah district in Pakistan

Earthquake damage in the mountains of Pakistan

Has Anyone Seen Osama?

n this post nine/eleven world, the mountains of Pakistan on the border of Afghanistan are dangerous places. This is the area where many of the terrorists are hiding out in caves. Once you see the terrain and the myriad of caves in the steep mountains, you realize why these terrorists can hide there and not get caught. We are interested in helping the poor in distress but our families were again concerned with the danger of our destination. After the October eighth earthquake, over one hundred thousand people died and it was estimated that over two million people were injured and most of these two million people became homeless. The governments of the world airlifted tents and supplies to these mountain people but no one went directly into the steep ravines and hillside dwellings of the villagers in their carved out towns in the Ghari Habibullah district.

"His Healing Hands" was asked if we would be willing to go to Muzafrabad, Pakistan and the Azaz, Kashmir area of the northwest frontier province to treat these people in their villages before the snow fell and made the roads impassable. Time was of the essence and lives were in the balance. It seems that God keeps stretching us and keeps preparing us in gradual stages to go where there is a human need. This continued expansion of our reliance on God for His protection and care has increased our faith and confidence and trust in Him. It has enabled us to better serve the disadvantaged peoples of the world.

We again partnered with Global Aid International Network and Campus Crusade for Christ under the leadership of Kenneth Shakeel, project manager from Islamabad. We slept in tents in a base camp that we set up on the grounds of Kunhar Hospital, keeping somewhat warm in long underwear and sleeping bags. It was an adventure to go to the bathroom at night in the freezing cold weather at eight thousand feet elevation. Every day we awoke, made a fire to warm up, drank hot coffee, prayed together and we loaded up four-wheel drive vehicles with our medicines, equipment, donated food and sweaters for distribution, and irrigation equipment to set up water filtration systems in the villages. We drove for several hours up into the steep mountain passes on narrow slippery roads to remote villages carved out of the hillsides.

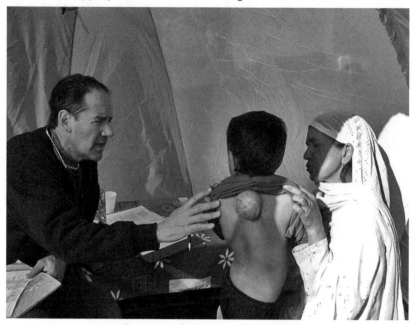

Treating a patient in an exam tent

The people were living in non-winterized tents and they greeted us with cheers and open arms.

These were very rugged people living in very jagged vertical mountains with barely drivable mountain passes. We were staying at only eight thousand feet but these mountains were the tallest mountains in the world, up to twenty- eight thousand feet. We could see glaciers in the distance. The roads were multiple switchbacks with huge boulders in the middle of the path. The villagers didn't travel on these "highways" but walked on goat paths and through the dry creek beds. Bob Dylan wrote that "the highway is for gamblers," and now I understand that verse. We set up tents for our clinics, and Ken Shakeel had brought translators from Islamabad to help in the pharmacy and with history taking and crowd control. After seeing all the patients in the village, we gave each family a sack of selected local foods to last them approximately one month. We also gave each person a warm sweater and we had a few winterized tents that we left with the headman of each village. During our clinic, another part of our team, helped set up a water filtration system that was fed by gravity drainage. The water was filtered through washed riverbed sand and small gravel into a polyethylene tank that we had brought up the mountain for each village we visited. After a full day of clinics, we left the villages before dusk so we could navigate the dangerous roads back to our base camp. We left these villagers with medicines, food, warm sweaters, tents, clean water, and loving kindness. They waved goodbye with glad, smiling, grateful faces and cheers. After another two-hour journey back to camp, we ate trail mix for dinner that we brought from home, crawled into our tents and fell asleep in seconds. This was the same exhausted, blissful sleep that I had experienced as a boy, falling asleep in summer camp in the Catskill Mountains of New York State. It is a strange mental experience when flashbacks of your youth invade your consciousness from the depths of your subconscious. I can even still smell the grass at dusk at that summer camp.

Due to my family's meager income, my mother enrolled me in Surprise Lake Camp for a two-week jaunt into the mountains, geared for poor families to get children off the hot, summer streets of New York City. The Eddie Cantor Foundation subsidized this camp, and my mother always said that it was cheaper to send me to camp than to feed me at home. At that age, I didn't live on trail mix and we all know how expensive it is to feed a teenager. This summer camp in the country was a complete change from the hot asphalt city streets. At night, you could actually see stars in the sky not blocked out by permanent city lights. I never knew that there were so many stars and the different smells and sounds of the country were completely unknown to me. I learned to swim in a lake, play baseball on real grass, sing around campfires, and sleep in a log cabin. I currently live on a ranch in the central coast of California, where I built a log cabin behind a lake. We make fires in our fire pit and cook outside as often as we can. My wife says that I have recreated my summer camp experiences. It was a time that even as a young boy, I reflected on questions about the meaning and origins of life. There is something about living outside, away from man-made edifices, that makes you think about the beginning of the world and where we fit into the majestic scheme of things or whether there actually is a blueprint or plan or grand design. I knew that life was finite because of the recent death of my father and when you view the sky, the earth, the sun, the moon and the stars; "the heavens declare the glory of God and the skies proclaim the work of His hands," it shouts of intelligent intention. Maybe that's why many of the great Old Testament biblical characters were shepherds like Abraham, David, and Moses, who lived outside and protected their sheep. They had time to reflect with only the sounds of the animals, and without the sounds of human speech or mechanical devices. I have spent a weekend in Death Valley at Zebrinski Point and the sound of silence is deafening. My mother, who has lived in New York City for eighty years can't sleep at night unless she hears sirens or fire trucks sometime during the night. Even now, she always sleeps with a radio blaring in the background. We need to be silent at times and listen and if we clear our mind, God will speak to us in some manner. To this day, when I look up at the sky, I feel the presence of God.

I remember walking in the woods on our ranch with my young daughter, Faith, and she asked me if we were lost. I told her that the world was round and therefore, you could never be truly lost if you kept walking straight ahead. This is a comical statement but it's true that we live on a globe and God is everywhere and always knows our location without a global positioning system. God is present in those mountains of Pakistan and in spite of the caves and hiding places, you can't hide from God. You may get off the path and think you're lost but God can find you at all times. These Pakistani villagers lived outside in these immense mountains tending their animals and I am sure they realized that only God could create this world of organization. We can calculate exactly when the sun will rise and set, when the moon will ascend and descend, when the planets will pass each other, and we can formulate a table to exactly predict the tides. These times are always accurate and never off by even a millisecond. Is this chance plus time or is there an "Organizer?"

We gave these villagers everything we had including a new fresh supply of clean water, free of bacteria, viruses, or parasites. This was accomplished by using the materials right in their area; all provided free

Polyethylene tank hauled up the mountain to supply clean fresh water

and in unlimited quantities from God's natural provision. Every morning, when we drove to each village, we had a leader who brought three
or four of the young men of the village down to the riverbed in the valley and fill bags with fresh washed sand and smooth rocks. We brought
the sand back to the village and repeatedly washed this sand with the
water from the village water supply. The team then drilled holes in the
polyethylene tank that we had hauled up the mountain and filled the
tank with this washed sand followed by the smooth river rock. All these
villages had a supply of water from the higher elevations and a plastic
pipe was fitted into the top of the tank. The water filtered through the
rocks and sand and then out a hole in the bottom of the tank fitted with
an outflow pipe. This system required two days to "charge" the system
and the result would be fresh clean water out the outflow pipe, free of
all pathogens. This method requires no pumps or electricity or moving
parts. It is simple, efficient and long lasting. In our medical clinic, we
provided medicines to treat parasites, and bacteria and this fresh clean
supply of water would keep the villagers free of water born disease. In
addition to the medical treatment and clean water, we supplied healthy

nutritious food donated by many of our supporters. We also had a very popular sweater company, donate thousands of warm sweaters. The style of these garments was not important but the warmth would save lives in the approaching winter cold months. These supplies and services were all provided in the love and care of the God that obviously created these amazing mountains. These people understood and we understood as well. God is love and this love is real. When you think of the conflicts in the world between different ethnic groups and different religions that have persisted for thousands of years, you realize that only God can eventually bring all peoples together with the only true common goal; the love of our Creator God for each and every one of us. This should translate into love for each other.

We have all been made in the image of God and stem from the same ancestry, which gives us a strong universal bond. We have historically emphasized our differences but our commonality is more ubiquitous and established than our discord and enmity. With the advent of DNA testing and identification in studying ethnic groups, we are seeing that our genetic similarities and our universality are more apparent than our diversity, which really points back to our shared lineage. If you read any newspaper in any language in any country of the world and you are a realist, you must come to the conclusion that man alone without God cannot solve his relationship problems. God has a plan and I'm glad that I have read the end of His book when His plan comes to fruition, because it gives me hope. Life without hope is depression. If you are not a believer and you lose everything in a hurricane, or an earthquake, or a Tsunami, you have indeed lost everything. But if you are a believer, you have Jesus and you still have everything.

When I discover a terminally ill patient in my private practice, I used to tell the patient the stark truth and the probability of their eminent outcome of death. I did this, not for lack of compassion, but I felt that it was my responsibility to the patient and the family to be as realistic as possible. As I have aged in my practice and my dealings with thousands of patients over thirty- five years, I have changed my approach to the terminally ill. They must have some hope, no matter how meager. I still present a realistic picture but I shroud it in hope and try to present alternatives that at least can extend life and the possibility of a cure no matter how remote. In doing this, patients and their families are happier, more optimistic, and the patients do live longer, just because of that hope. The best hope is an eternal life with God. This alternative is not available to all; not because it is not offered freely, but because it is not accepted unreservedly by all. God is not selective and makes His offer of eternal life to everyone, based on the free will acceptance of God the Son. God gave us free will and He will not violate or invade our free will or treat us like puppets on a string. Before I was a believer, I used to think patients believed just because it made it easier for them to die, and their belief was just escapism. I have observed as a doctor, that believers in the living God, who have assurance of eternal life, do live and die with more peace and joy then non-believers. However, this is not based on a need or excuse, but is a result of their belief. It is founded on the truth or it wouldn't be believable. People will live for a false cause but they will never die for a false cause. It became very obvious to our group concerning man's inability to live in harmony with his fellow man, when we traveled to Kashmir. The earthquake plays no favorites and doesn't respect borders of countries.

Pakistanis with bags of donated food

On our last clinic day, we traveled to Kashmir on the Pakistani side of the border, as Kashmir is divided between India and Pakistan. We went through multiple border checks and for the first time they didn't mind Americans as long as we were not of Indian descent. The Kashmiri people whether they are Indian or Pakistani look and sound the same. Their dress is indistinguishable, and yet they love to hate each other. Without God, their century old feud doesn't seem to have a chance at reconciliation. The God of the Bible is a God of reconciliation. God the Father sent His Son, Jesus to reconcile us to Him. We traveled up the beautiful Kashmiri Mountains to treat village people who had lost everything: their loved ones, their homes and all their possessions. Kashmir is said to be paradise and it truly is beautiful, but the feuding peoples have made it a fallen paradise.

We went through our usual routine of setting up our clinic tents, with our various stations of intake history, vital signs and blood sugars, medical doctors with translators, and pharmacy. We treated the people all day without a break, as our lines were endless. We gave everyone vitamins, dewormed the children, and treated a lot of infections, with an eye on the forthcoming cold winter months. While I was administering to these people, I watched children driving donkeys with water containers to the local cistern in front of our clinic setup. They led these donkeys to the well and the women of the village drew the water. It reminded me of the woman at the well in Samaria whom Jesus confronted at Jacob's well. Jesus offered her "living" water and she wanted this "living" water, as she thought that she wouldn't have to daily draw the regular water from the well. She didn't understand that Jesus was offering her eternal life. Jesus told her that she didn't understand what a wonderful gift God was offering her. When we offer people medicine, it is up to them whether or not they accept and trust our medicines and whether they will avail themselves of its benefit. These villagers were given almost all that we had to offer. They gladly took our medicines, the sweaters, the food and the new water filtration system and we attempted to witness to them about Jesus by our words and our actions of supplying their physical needs. They loved our supplies but most of them didn't comprehend the offer of "living" water. Our host, Ken, had assured us that since we had been allowed in this area for the first time, he and a team of believers would now to able to return to the village to share "the rest of the story." God offers and everyone must decide for themselves whether to accept or reject the free offer, as a very personal decision. As a medical missionary organization, we get a lot of secondary gain and good feelings from the people we serve, but there is also sadness concerning the people that don't understand what they are rejecting and the consequences of their decision. The sadness, however, is overpowered by the joy of service to God and His people, the sowing of seeds in the hearts of needy people, and the inexplicable elation for the ones that do believe. These emotions and feelings, knowledge and understanding, and our faith in the God of Abraham, Isaac, and Jacob, will continue to keep us on the medical mission field. Some of these medical trips were under difficult conditions, but our medical missionary trip to Fiji was a complete joy and it was as if we had a protective guide going before us to prepare the way. When the children of Israel left pharaoh's Egypt, they were accompanied by God in the form of a cloud by day to block the scorching, searing heat of the sun, and a fire by night to give them light and warmth in the freezing desert night air. They were always aware of God being at the forefront, and they only traveled in the desert when the cloud or the fire moved before them. From the beginning to the end of our trip to Fiji, every potential problem was converted to a blessing; every obstacle was changed to an opportunity; and every difficulty was changed to a delight. It was as if God was leading us with a cloud by day and a fire by night.

Patients waiting their turn in a "His Healing Hands" medical clinic in Fiji.

"Hear no evil, see no evil, and say no evil." Our medical team in Fiji, Our M.D., our Chief Operating Officer and our Pharmacist

You Meant It To Harm But God Meant It For Good

We left for the Islands of Fiji at midnight on the red eye and traveled through the night and into the day crossing the international dateline. Every door seemed to be opened before us, including treating over one thousand four hundred patients, being allowed to preach in the Fijian and Indian churches, and giving our testimonies for God while we changed reels during the showing of the Jesus film. We were able to go to very remote villages, deep in the jungle where the chief told us that we were the first missionary group to ever come to help them. We went to another village on the island of Tavauni where the king allowed us to treat his subjects after we performed certain mandatory rituals.

Our adventure really began when we learned that one of our doctor's flights had been moved up four hours and we couldn't get in touch with him. It wasn't possible for him and his family to arrive at the airport on time for the flight. We were flying half way around the world with a full schedule of clinic commitments on different islands. If this doctor, who was an integral part of our team, didn't arrive on time and we had to wait for him or proceed without him, it would literally be disastrous. In addition, each team member had to check one seventy-pound bag of medicines. These medicine bags had been packed with different medicines to treat different diseases. He was traveling with his wife, a nurse and his two children. We would have missed a doctor, a nurse and four bags of important medicines. We got the news about his early flight while we were driving from the central coast of California to Los Angeles International Airport; a four hour drive. We tried to contact him but to no avail. I was driving my truck with five others and a long bed full of suitcases in the rain. It seemed as if we were off to a very rocky start. One of the passengers led us in prayer. Just at the end of his prayer, my cell phone rang. Jeff's wife, who was home manning the phones, got in touch with our doctor's nurse in his office and found him shopping for the trip with his wife and two children. They had called the airlines but couldn't arrive in time for the updated flight. They had originally been scheduled for a different flight than the rest of our group because of lack of seating on our flight. The airlines changed their flight to our exact airplane without being aware of our team. Now we all would fly together with a better time schedule then previously booked. God had changed a bad situation that we had arranged into a better situation that He arranged. He does this all the time and often times we are not aware of the circumstances. This principal reminds me of a much more drastic change of circumstances in the Bible story of Joseph and his brothers.

While I continued to drive my truck to Los Angeles International airport, I kept thinking of the words of Joseph to his brothers in the Bible, "You meant evil against me, but God meant it for good."

Joseph was his father Jacob's favorite son and his brothers knew it and were naturally jealous of him. When Joseph was singled out by his father with a coat of many colors, their envy and jealousy turned to rage. Then, Joseph told his brothers of a dream he had, where his entire family including his brothers would bow down to him. They couldn't live with this dreamer any longer and decided to kill him, but his brother, Reuben, convinced them to throw him into a cistern, in order to save his life. Reuben planned to rescue him later but his brothers sold him to a passing caravan. Joseph was sold into slavery, elevated to a level of responsibility in his master's house but later thrown into jail due to his master's wife's lying about Joseph's advances toward her. Although Joseph was in jail, God had not forgotten about him. When the Pharaoh had a dream, Joseph was called upon to interpret the Pharaoh's dream, as a former cellmate knew that Joseph could interpret dreams. Joseph told the Pharaoh that only God could interpret his dream. God gave Joseph the answer to the Pharaoh's dream and as a result, the Pharaoh made Joseph the second highest official, beside himself in all of Egypt, in charge of all the food stores in the land.

There was a famine in the land, and Joseph's father sent his brothers to get food so they could survive because the continued existence of the entire line of God's chosen people was in grave peril. God uses Joseph to "save" his family and reunite them. After the death of Jacob, Joseph's brothers were afraid that Joseph would take revenge on them for what they had done to him. Joseph said to them, "Don't be afraid. You intended to harm me, but God intended it for good to accomplish what is now being done, the saving of many lives."

God uses the plans of devious men and turns them around to advance His Kingdom for good. In my life, I have seen this happen many times. My well-laid plans go astray and I begin to worry and complain, but God has a better plan and uses the circumstances to reverse the burden to become a blessing. The recent terrible mining deaths may help to change the laws to safeguard and save many future miners. The horrible threat of nuclear holocaust may force men to make treaties for peace. Even the atrocious three thousand deaths of September eleventh, may change history for the good. Sometimes it is hard for us to see the potential good in the hands of God that change the evil acts of man. God is not the author of sin but He can bail us out when we trust in Him. Jesus Christ's most horrible death by crucifixion was the worst thing that man has ever done to God, but the substitutionary death of Jesus for our sins, followed by His resurrection was the most gracious act of God to save man for eternity, and the best thing God has ever done for man.

By the time our little missionary group traveled to Fiji, we had been in enough previous circumstances to at least partially trust in God's providential care. We were now all on the same flight to Fiji, excited at the opportunity that God had given us to treat, preach and teach, the poor people of Fiji. Although I experienced God's direct intervention in rearranging our travel itinerary to our benefit, I was worried about my own health. Several days before we left for Fiji, I had injured the bottom of my right foot and it became infected. I started to take antibiotics, soaked my foot, and applied hydrogen peroxide and antibiotic cream. I knew that it would heal but I was unable to wear a shoe on my right foot, and I was worried that the heat and humidity of Fiji would wreak havoc with my foot if I wore an occlusive shoe. In the airplane, I was able to take my shoe off, but what was I going to do in Fiji while seeing patients if I was to show respect to these people. If only I would learn to completely rely on God even for the little "stuff." Again, God had already solved my problem. Culturally, the people in Fiji take off their shoes when they enter into any house or indoor enclosure and after clinics we were able to swim in the beautiful Pacific Ocean. Leaving my shoes off during our clinics and swimming in the Ocean in the evening healed my foot very quickly. I needed to trust God in everything, even in the little details. I began to relax as we approached the beautiful resort Islands of Fiji.

It is really an amazing contrast that in a resort area where wealthy people spend a lot of money, there are always very destitute people. We came to spread God's love to them through medical care. Fiji is breathtakingly beautiful, with warm balmy weather and wonderful coral seas teaming with life. The native people are extremely friendly but very needy of medical care and God's love. There are two distinct ethnic groups; Native Fijians and Indians from India who were brought to the Islands as a labor force. Their customs are different, their food is completely diverse, their body habitus are poles apart, and their diseases are totally dissimilar. The Indians had a lot of hypertension, hypercholesterolemia, and were markedly obese. The Fijians were thin, more athletic, but had a

Our Fijian medical team of doctors, nurses, pharmacists and para-medical assistants

lot of infections, gastritis and arthritis. People are different but really all the same. They need love, peace, joy, family ties, and a belief in God. We came to Fiji to share with them and they also shared with us.

Our hosts from Campus Crusade for Christ were delighted to see us, as not many medical teams come to Fiji. Our plans were to set up medical clinics in the courtyards of both Fijian and Indian churches, and to have clinics in remote villages. Our first clinic was on the Island of Vita Levu in the city of Nandi. We set up our clinic outside a Fijian church on the grass and the wind began to pick up and it began to rain. The people were very used to this warm rain but it was becoming difficult to evaluate these people properly. I noticed that the pastor and some of his elders were off on the side praying. The wind seemed to blow the clouds away very rapidly and the sun came out to begin a beautiful balmy pleasant day. A large crowd started to gather and mill around while they waited for various medical stations and to get their medicines that we prescribed. Since we were so busy medically, we didn't have time to speak to the people about our motivation of coming to the island to tell them and show them the love of God through medicine. As the crowd enlarged we worried about keeping them content and occupied. Then, a large group of young students from Campus Crusade for Christ showed up at our clinic. It seemed that they were looking for something to do and they heard about us. They started playing with the kids and making balloons and giving out tracts in the Fijian language and witnessing to the people. It was a carnival atmosphere, while the physical and emotional and spiritual needs of the people were met, in a beautiful setting with exquisite weather on one of the loveliest islands of the world. The people were delighted and the church was excited about all the people of the community finding their location, as a great many of the patients inquired about the church services. People respond when you reach out to them in love and give them a free will offering in the name of Jesus. Everyone was blessed that glorious day. Our medicines were appropriate and needed, the Campus Crusade for Christ young people had a wonderful, joyous experience of sharing the gospel with the citizenry, and the people were administered to in the name of God. It couldn't have been orchestrated any better than if God did it Himself and I think He did coordinate that entire day. There is a special feeling when you sense that you are in the will of God: in the right place at the right time. When this happens, God's love is on display and the recipients fall more and more in love with God. We continued to have clinics like this and it seemed to rain everyday but the clouds parted during our clinic times. It was a tremendous coincidence; or was it?

After several more daily clinics, we traveled around the other side of the island to the city of Suva. We held another clinic and the workers of our hotel, including the front desk workers, the chamber maids, the cleaning crew and all the service people heard that we were medical personnel and asked us to treat them. We held another mini-clinic in the hotel lobby and treated hundreds of grateful, poor hotel workers. We had a great time and the hotel service naturally was spectacular for us after that clinic. We served and again were served. This is what life should be about, with everyone helping each other. On Sunday, I was given the privilege of preaching the sermon in one of the Indian churches.

I love to preach in the churches of foreign countries with a translator because cultural differences are completely bridged by the love of God. It is really fun and inspiring to hear the same Christian songs that we sing in a different language, extolling the identical Jesus. I discussed the verse that tells about Jesus going about all the cities and villages, preaching the word of God, teaching about the Kingdom of God, and healing every kind of disease and every sickness. That's the verse we try to emulate and it is the verse that our medical missionary group is based upon. The people responded with joy and gladness and we had a wonderful time of fellowship. Many of our medical team were able to give their personal testimonies and this blessed them, as well. Many of the Indian people in the church were there for the first time since they had been drawn to the church by our medical clinics the previous days. The next day, we sched-

Doctors and local translators

uled a day of rest and recuperation and charted a boat to go snorkeling, scuba diving, and swimming on an isolated, pristine white sand beach.

As usual, it rained but only when we were snorkeling, which brought all the beautiful fish around our boat. One of our team hitched a ride on a giant tortoise and another member of the team went scuba diving off a fantastically colored reef. When we arrived at "our" island, the sun shown and when we went back to the boat, it started to rain again. We were getting the idea that God was going before us. The rain was beautiful, but the approaching storm behind us was very threatening. We beat the storm into port and just before we arrived, we went under a double completely intact rainbow. Some of the team actually cried with the joy of this display from God.

The following day we boarded a small prop plane to the idyllic island of Tavauni directly on the International Date Line. We had conditionally arranged to hold a clinic in a village where we needed the approval of the headman of the village, who rarely allowed outsiders to view their secret traditions or fellowship with their people. The evening before our visit, we received some instructions from the village liaison.

We were instructed in bowing and never approaching the king unless we were approaching on our knees. This created a very strange feeling in me, because as an American, equality for all people has always been ingrained in me. As a Jew, I have been taught not to bow down to idols or make gods of other people. As a Christian, I knew that the only one who deserves this kind of homage is the Lord. However, we agreed to obey the cultural rules of the tribe in order to demonstrate the love of the only one true God. It turned out that these rules were only looked upon as humility and ritualistic historical cultural rites. The next day we were greeted by our contact person and taken to the official greeting hall. We received further instructions of what to say and how to act including accepting a bowl of cava if it was offered to us as a sign of friendship and personal approval. I had heard of cava but I didn't know about its ingredients. I was about to find out all about its effects.

Jeff Walker sharing his testimony in church.

We entered the hall after removing our shoes, and sat on the floor with legs crossed, waiting for the elders of the court and their King. We were all a little nervous. While we waited, I started to think about what it would be like to approach the thrown of the real King of the universe. Would I be like Isaiah who said, "Woe is me," or like Peter, when he realized that Jesus was God said, "Get away from me for I am a sinner," or would I approach God with the confidence of the knowledge that Jesus is my advocate in heaven? My thoughts were interrupted by the advent of the "king and his court." We kept our eyes down as we had been instructed and quietly awaited for the elders to finish talking to the king. They passed the cava bowl around to each elder and then one at a time; we crawled on our knees to approach the king, bowed again and drank from the cava bowl. I am always very careful about eating and drinking on these medical trips because I can't afford to get sick due to my medical responsibilities to our patients and the rest of the team. But this was a perfect way to spread infection and my lips began to tingle and become numb. I later found out that cava contains a compound that acts as an anesthetic and a narcotic derivative, which incidentally and advantageously killed the bacteria being spread by all the elders and the king, to us. I would never have agreed to any of this if I didn't feel that this was in the will and protection of God.

We had all performed our ritualistic homage and were accepted to get a tour of the village with the king and to set up our medical clinic. We held our medical clinic and treated everyone in the village, about two hundred of the tribesmen, some of which had never seen a medical

The "King" of the village is served by the elders of the village around the Cava bowl.

doctor. Toward the end of the clinic, even the king became one of my patients and he was so grateful for our care that he invited me back to sit around in the circle of elders with him and "enjoy" stories of our lives and imbibe in more cava. The king shared a story of how he had served with the Australian Army during World War Two. It turned out that he was very proud of a citation he had received from the United States Army. It was my turn to share through a translator. I gave my testimony of how I sought God all my life as a Jewish believer and finally came to salvation by a knowledge and recognition of Jesus as the Jewish Messiah, who died for everyone, even the king and the elders and his tribesmen. They listened attentively and asked a few questions. They were interested and our hosts in Campus Crusade said they would now be able to follow up with this village, which they had never before been able to enter. In order to leave the circle of cava drinkers, I had to get one of our team members to take my place, as I couldn't handle any more of the cava and still treat patients. God does work in mysterious ways, even around a cava bowl.

We left the beautiful island of Tavauni after we went to the International Date Line and kept crossing the date line going from Saturday to Sunday and back again to Saturday on the same day. I guess small things

Bill Walker, our senior staff member, whose joy and love for people leads us in the proper giving attitude. He mercifully replaced me at the cava bowl.

occupy small minds. We held our last clinic in a very remote village in the middle of a jungle, which we approached in four-wheel drive vehicles. We set up the clinic in the village leader's house and showed the Jesus film to the people waiting in line. It was very surreal for me to occasionally glimpse up at the screen and see Jesus healing the people while we were giving them medicines to heal their physical problems. The people in the line were getting the gospel on the screen in their own language and they were very interested. Our team gave their individual testimonies during the changing of the reels of the film, and the head of the village told me that we were the first missionary group of any kind to offer help to his people. Many of these people were diagnosed with diabetes, including

One of the Fijian families we were able to treat and
share the love of God

the headman. None of them knew that they had diabetes as they had never before had their blood sugar drawn. We arranged for medical follow up through our indigenous translators, and the people assured us they would pursue this care. These villagers treated us as if we were royalty and were amazed by our efforts, compassion and expression of love, which we told them came from God. They had been exposed to the love of God for the first time and they were very affected by this expression of irresistible affection.

This entire trip was perfect and it was obvious to all of us that it had been orchestrated by the God of the Bible. We initially started "His Healing Hands" to treat patients, teach about Jesus, and preach the gospel. We were also interested in uplifting indigenous pastors in the eyes of their congregation. We wanted a Christian organization that allowed non-Christians to participate in humanitarian medical care and be a witness to them as well. We later added disaster relief to our plans as a result of the leading of God, based on the needs of people all over the world. In summary, we wanted to do the will of God and be in the will of God and demonstrate and reflect His love. I believe God has accomplished all these goals and He has brought all of us closer to Him. I have written all these things down in the hope of exposing others to God through our experiences, and with the further trust that it will encourage them to seek after the God of the Bible with an open heart and mind.

"A Prophet is Never Recognized in His Own Town"

have traveled all over the world, including six continents; teaching, preaching, giving my testimony of what I have seen and heard, treating thousands of patients, but the most difficult group of people that I have ever witnessed to, is my own family. I traveled to New York City for my mother's ninetieth birthday celebration, staying up late into many of the nights discussing our need for the God of the Bible to my sister, my mother, and my brother-in-law. My mother doesn't travel and I rarely get to go to New York City, and as a result, I felt an immediacy to not only enjoy my mother's company, but to acknowledge the God of the Bible; their God of Abraham, Isaac, and Jacob. I considered this visit a great success, not because of convincing anyone of this necessity, but because I spoke of God to my family without insulting anyone. For me, that was a big accomplishment. My family has always thought that I have gone off the deep end. It is really understandable, as a Jew doesn't usually believe in Jesus as the Messiah. A New York city- dweller doesn't leave New York to become a California farmer in a rural setting, and a Jewish doctor doesn't travel to Moslem counties talking to many Moslems about the love and peace of Jesus, while trying to meet their physical needs with free medicines. It is interesting that most of the poor people that we treat are Moslems and many of my American colleagues in light of terrorism ask me why we bother to help Moslems. God calls us to tell the good news to everyone. In learning to love man, especially the unlovable, we learn to love God, who created all men with some of His attributes.

I came to New York City to celebrate my mother's ninety years of living and to celebrate the God that has granted her these ninety years. We must rejoice and commemorate both, as they are inseparable. I often feel the presence of God in my daily routine, and I acknowledge God in guiding and leading me in this daily walk. My mother and sister say that they feel a spirit or a force in their lives but they only recognize themselves in controlling their actions. In fact, they get upset at the suggestion that any entity outside of their own thoughts and actions could have any effect on controlling their lives. They feel that they are in complete control, giving themselves credit for all the good that befalls them but for the "evil," they feel that they are unlucky or victims of circumstance. I believe in the providence of God combined with the free will of man. I don't completely understand this amalgamation, but I know that they both exist separately and jointly.

My mother, my sister, and my brother-in-law

My family repeatedly tells me not to bring up the name of Jesus or talk about His ministry and in the next breath they ask me to clarify what I believe is my relationship to God. My mother can't help herself because she doesn't have the answers to life, even after living ninety years of introspection. In fact, it is this looking inward that has given them a lack of answers and confusion. My sister is Jewish and goes to temple. She believes in Jewish mysticism, called the Cabala. She turned to Buddhism for contentment and now has delved into Zen-Buddhism at the advise of her Jewish Rabbi. If this isn't confusing enough, she meditates to eliminate suffering, and purges herself of all desires in an effort to find Nirvana that she does desire. When I questioned my sister, asking very simple questions about her belief system, she either gives very unintelligible, complex answers, using intricate, complicated words to explain; which in fact, camouflages the details, or she says, "my Rashi could explain this, but I can't." When I explain Christianity in very simple, straightforward terminology, she states "Buddhism and Christianity are very similar." She uses my same vocabulary but not my same dictionary. The words are identical but their meanings have been fashioned to her agenda. The world has changed the meaning of words to fit into their secular, anti-religious attitudes. In truth, Buddhism and Christianity are opposites. Buddhism is looking inward to find the self in order to lose the self, while Christianity is looking outward to the Creator to understand the self via The Maker who knows most about us because He designed us. I believe that an arrangement needs an arranger, an organization needs an organizer, and it is my gut feeling that a design needs a designer. She is looking internally, and I am looking externally. Superficially, it would seem logical to look inward to understand oneself but only if you are both the creator and the created. The watch can't heal itself. Only the watchmaker knows the inner workings of the watch. A clay pot doesn't understand itself or other pots; only the potter understands pottery. My sister trusts in Cabalism, Buddhism, and Zen Buddhism. I trust in God. When I call to God, He is always there for me. Although I fall short and disappoint God, he has never disappointed me.

We both acknowledge suffering in the world. Suffering is universal. She relates it to good and bad karma. I relate it to sin in the world and man's inherent selfishness. She believes that suffering is the result of desires and these desires must be eliminated by right views, right speech, right conduct, and right mind control through meditation to eradicate the self by the self. I believe God can use suffering to bring us closer to Him, although He is not the author of this suffering. She believes that enlightenment by creating a state of nothingness leads to Nirvana. I believe Heaven is being with God, which can only be accomplished through our relationship with Jesus the Son, who paid the price in full for our sins. She looks to self, as she is on the throne of her life. I look to God my Creator; who is on the throne of my life. My sister wants contentment and inner peace and feels that during meditation, she can transiently achieve her goal. The problem is that she always returns to the real world and discontentment. God is my contentment; my peace; my faith; and He never changes and is always available. I love my sister, my mother and my brother-in-law, and I pray that they would find inner peace and contentment, but they will have to do it by the Way, the Truth, and the Life. For my sister or anyone else to have inner peace, first you need peace with God, before you can have the peace of God. This peace with God can only come about if we accept His

Son, Jesus as our Lord and Savior. How can we ever accept the death of a child, the loss of a loving mate, or our own permanent disability if we only rely on our own wavering peace? We need the peace of God through Jesus the Son. This peace of God is available through prayer, thanksgiving, and supplication through Jesus.

Sometimes, I wish there were many ways to get to heaven, but I didn't write the Book, and my way would have been unfair and not impartial. Everyone is equal in God's eyes and has an equal chance to come to Him through His Son. God has done all the work, from start to finish, regardless of our intellect, our money, our social status, or any of our abilities. No one has any advantage, and all we have to do is believe in the Jesus of the Bible. It says that we should not boast in our wisdom, or our strength, or our riches, but that we should boast that we understand and know God. Jesus sacrificed for us and to know Him is to know God.

He fulfilled prophecy. He performed miracles in front of eyewitnesses. He changes lives; He changed mine. Jesus will accept you the way you are, but will not leave you the way you were. His story is history verified by archaeological discoveries. He lived a sinless life and paid the price of our sins, and He offers eternity with God the Father as a free gift. What could be more universal or simple or fair? I have been accused of being a dogmatic, right-wing Christian and asked, "What makes you think that your way is the only way?" It is not my way, it is God's way and God is never wrong. Truth is always dogmatic and rejects all falsehoods.

I have used my sister's belief in Buddhism as a contrast to Christianity, but this contrast can be made with all the religions of the world. I challenge the Jewish Rabbis of today to explain the book of Isaiah, Psalms 2, 22, 45, 72, and finally Psalm 110 without relating them to Jesus of Nazareth; the true Messiah. When the leaders of the Jews tried to trick Jesus with complex theological questions, He turned the tables on them by asking them, what they thought was a very simplistic question. Jesus asked them, "What do you think about the Christ?" "Whose son is he?" They thought the answer was easy. They replied, "The son of David." Jesus asked them, "Then why did David call him Lord in Psalm 110?" "The Lord says to my Lord: Sit at my right hand." The true answer that they refused to state was that He was both human; the son of David, and divine; the Son of God. Jesus had claimed to be both in the line of David, through Mary and Joseph, and the Son of God through the Holy Spirit. Jews educated in the Jewish scriptures today, know that their scriptures repeatedly state that only God can forgive sins and save people to give them eternal life, and yet they also know that their Word speaks of a kinsman redeemer, a man to save them. It is obvious in reading the Bible that the Messiah, (the Savior), must be both God and man and yet the Rabbis to this day refuse to acknowledge this simple biblical principal scattered throughout their entire Jewish scriptures.

Mormonism, Jehovah's Witnesses, and Islam can claim that Jesus is only a prophet or one of the gods but their own scriptures contradict these views.

Even today many Christian denominations create a false impression of Jesus. At Christmas, we see Jesus as a baby in a manger. He is no longer in a manger. At Easter, we see Jesus on the cross. He is no longer on the cross. Jesus is sitting on the right hand of God the Father. We, believers need to understand this, in order for us to understand our relationship to Him. He is not a baby or suffering on a cross. His work is complete and His position of sitting on the right hand of the Father indicates this completed work and His equal co-reign with God the Father. In the future, He will judge the world and every one of us, based on our belief in Him. We either believe Him or deny Him.

I was invited to give the Christian viewpoint in a panel discussion with an Islamic representative and a Jewish Rabbi concerning the world situation and "bridging the gap" between the major religions of the world. I was very encouraged by this invitation as the forum was arranged by the students of a local high school. We discussed our similarities, commonalities, and differences with a goal of at least opening up communication. We took statements from the audience and I was amazed at one particular proclamation by a gentleman who introduced himself as being Jewish. He boldly and unabashedly declared that the answer to bridging the gap between the religions and the Middle East problems was very simple and obvious. He said that God needed an eleventh commandment; "Live and let live." I was amazed that God had left out a commandment. Can you imagine that? I didn't reply to this comment but I questioned in my mind, what this man's relationship was to the God of the universe. He must have considered God his buddy, just as human as him. No culture ever rose higher than their idea of God. God is God and the gulf between man and God is infinite. God doesn't make mistakes or omit anything. We cannot add or detract from God in any way. God has provided us with everything that we need to know

Him and come to Him. Our problem is not God. Our problems stem from our relationship to Him and to each other. Man will never solve the Middle East quagmire but God will resolve our dilemma. I know this because I have read the end of "The Book." I am frequently asked questions about the Bible to purposely stump me and emphasize so called apparent inconsistencies in the Bible. I do have several unanswerable questions myself, that I will ask Jesus when I get to heaven, but as a wise man once said, "If your God is so small as to be completely understood by man, then He is not large enough to be worshiped." Many people love to worship themselves. That is not enough for me. I love to worship God.

My sister separated religious belief in Buddhism from the application of the principles of meditation and denial of desires. That enables her to follow the precepts of Buddhism and continue to follow the rituals of Judaism. Christians cannot separate belief from application. They do not have that luxury. Jesus cannot be your Savior if He is not also your Lord. We can read our Bibles; memorize scripture; and quote chapter and verse; but if we don't apply this knowledge to our lives, it is a futile exercise in self-indulgence and the epitome of arrogance. Christian belief demands action and changed lives. My changed life and your changed life is a witness that Jesus exists and is in control today.

Life is about glorifying God and not ourselves. Christianity is not about working your way to heaven by good works or meditation. It is about a relationship to God. It is personal, active, and costly. Jesus paid the price but He wants the only thing we can give, our lives. Works cannot save us, but a saved man will want and yearn to do good works. God wants us to love Him and love each other. This love is a sacrificial love, and it requires that we put God and others first and subjugate our own needs to others needs. Plato believed that we could separate intellect from righteousness. Alexander The Great believed that we could find God emotionally through mysticism, music, incense and chanting. We are both intellect and emotion, and knowledge of God must be personal and practical, intellectual and emotional, filling the mind as well as the heart. It is both an idea and a personal relationship with Jesus, who is fully God and became fully man by taking on human form and we can follow Him as a personal example.

Sometimes it is hard to accept new or different ideas because we get set in our ways and feel uncomfortable with change. At times we must back up before we can go forward. My wife's old Greek grandmother taught my wife to sew and in her needlework instructions gave her a very important principle of life. She said, "To be a good sewer, you need to know when to go back and rip out stitches that are wrong, and you must do it to create a good finished job." Sometimes we know when things are illogical or unfounded, but we refuse to rip out the stitches that we worked so hard to place, even when we know that they are incorrect. Throughout the Bible, God states that if we seek Him with an open mind and heart, He will reveal Himself to us. God can help us rip out stitches that separate us from Him and help us become the people we were originally created to be. This is true of believers as well as non-believers. I experienced this ripping out of stitches on a very intimate, frightening and upsetting level when I led a group on a return trip to India.

I love the people of India, but their spirituality without the knowledge and faith of Jehovah God saddens me. Although they are one billion strong, I feel very lonely when I am in India. During my first trip to India, I experienced what I considered a miraculous physical rebirth from the clutches of death by the prayers of my prayer support team back home. I have previously described how our small group in a taxi "should" have died on the road to Hyderabad. This time, my predicament and personal catastrophe was worse because it involved a very deep rooted, fearful, private emotional anxiety that has been with me all my life and rears it's terrifying head periodically.

I have always said and felt that I was a "loner," not needing other people and desiring time alone. This is true in part as I spend a lot of time with people as a doctor, a teacher, a farmer, a husband and a parent, and I require some time to just be still, watch the grass grow, and listen to the Lord. I grew up in a big city with people all around me and have traveled to very dense, highly populated cities to treat the poor. I am very comfortable with these crowds but at times yearn to be alone with my own thoughts, doing nothing. I love to walk in the hills of my ranch with my dogs and my thoughts, with human voices silenced, feeling the dirt yielding under my feet with the sky and clouds painted above. My dogs are good companions but I can't get them to appreciate a sunrise or a sunset, believe me, I've tried. They would rather chase a squirrel or a rabbit.

I led a group of medical personnel of "His Healing Hands" missionary organization, in a third return trip to India, as the medical needs of the poor in India are endless. Since we now have a web site, hishealinghands.com, all of these people were new to our team but very eager and competent. We had a very successful medical trip, treating thousands of needy Indians. I was delighted with our teams competency, proficiency, teamwork, and compassionate care, but I felt terribly alone in the midst of thousands of people. When I went to sleep in my room at night, I wasn't able to sleep and I had an old sinking feeling that I had experienced as a young boy. My father died when I was eight years old and since that time, I have had this sinking feeling of aloneness and fear of death and it's unknown experience, when I would awaken in the middle of the night. This feeling returned to me in India due to jet lag and sleep deprivation. The traveling to India is very arduous and takes an entire weekend with airtime, connections and layovers. The time difference from my home in California to India is ten and a half hours. I still can't figure out where the half hour comes from, but the travel and time change plus crossing the International Date Line can be very confusing to our internal clock and diurnal cycle. I was unable to sleep on the planes or in the airport terminals for forty-eight hours and I needed to be rested to lead my team and function as a medical doctor. This combination of tiredness, sleep deprivation, and fear of not being at my best, created a situation where my defenses and subconscious fears invaded my conscious awareness just before I would go to bed at night.

I am a very active, responsible person and these feelings of fear, loneliness, and dread were horrifying to me and I questioned my sanity. These are emotions that I have counseled others about and now I was the one that needed the help due to panicking and feeling that I wouldn't be able to sleep. The only way that I could get to sleep after hours of wakefulness, being hot then cold and clammy with a racing heart, was to take an antihistamine, called Benadryl. This worked but made me feel groggy in the mornings, and it wasn't a solution to my problem. I was functioning adequately during the day but my joy was missing. I decided to stop taking the medicines and got on my knees to pray to my Father in heaven, through Jesus His Son. Each night, the only thing that would calm my heart was the thought of Jesus and that He was my advocate and was always there for me; and He was there for me. I read my Bible and prayed for mental salvation. I prayed for serenity and the alleviation of my fears, my emptiness, and my loneliness. I had never allowed myself to experience these terrifying feelings for more than a few minutes, and had camouflaged them with activity. The cat was out of the bag and I decided to use this fearful experience to deal with this sublimated awful mind-set, and rid myself of this terror once and for all. I prayed each night and read my Bible. I read Daniel's prayer of confession for his people and himself while God's people were in captivity in Babylon. I was in captivity and I wanted to be free of this loneliness. I realized that I had been serving out of selfishness and empty conceit, and had wronged my saved brethren, unsaved people and most of all God. I confessed all this and prayed a prayer that I never thought that I would ever pray. I prayed to love and need people, and consider others more important then myself. This idea that I was a loner and relied only on myself without needing others, only worked when I was physically healthy without ailments that compromised my abilities. I have always taken care of myself, and as a doctor, I have administered to patients in their dependent state and couldn't imagine being dependent myself and certainly never lonely. But now I was lonely and I did need other people and my prayer to need and rely on others was the most foreign idea to me that I had ever contemplated. I slept that night and the dread and emptiness gradually, steadily subsided. I had never fully allowed myself to get into these feelings or shared these emotions with anyone and they festered in my brain for fifty years. Before I became a believer, my self-image was purely based on my own personal accomplishments and successes in education, possessions, and relationships. Certainly there have also been failures but I have always relied on my own initiative to bail myself out of trouble. As a believer, I have come to base my self-image on the fact that God loves me and sacrificed for me. If God thinks that I am worthwhile, then who am I to disagree or doubt Him? This positive image must be tempered with my knowledge that I am a sinner and I must be humble before the God of the universe, with all good things coming from Him and not me. As I have become more aware of the awesome holiness, righteousness, and amazing loving kindness of God, I have become more "sin sensitive." My walk with God has become more intimate and personal and as I get closer to God, my sinful nature has become more apparent to me. I have been in the company of faithful men and women who have given their all to God in a sacrificial manner. I am repeatedly amazed that God is willing to use me, when I compare myself to these godly people. So you see, I can now only rely on God for my self-image and not my own accomplishments that don't exist apart from the God of the universe. When I start to doubt and become unsure, I realize that my unsteady feeling is my mind and not God. God is stronger than my wavering, vacillating mind and my assurance returns to me due to my thoughts of His unchanging nature.

God is always there for me, but I must trust in Him. If I am worrying, I am not trusting, and if I am trusting, then I am not worrying. It's not whether I have a problem. It's whether the problem has me.

I would love to tell you that now I never have these thoughts or feelings since God dealt with my emotions, but that is not true. What is true is that these thoughts and my fearful emotions are much less in intensity and frequency and when they occur, we deal with them: God and me. I am never alone as long as I realize God is always with me and will never abandon me. I need God and I assume everyone else does as well. I have peace with God, but at times I don't have peace with myself. The power of the peace of God is greater than the weakness of my own agitation and anxiety. Death is of course still an unknown and anything that is mysterious and unidentifiable will always cause trepidation. But Jesus has said that He goes to the Father to prepare a place for me and I believe Him. I can't imagine what I would do during times of fear if I didn't have God. I can't envision living a life with all it's problems and ups and down without being able to talk to God, pray to God asking for His help, and relying on His availability to aid and comfort me. When we die, we leave with God or with nothing. In fact, we all have God, if we allow Him to come into our lives, and avail ourselves of what our Father offers to us.

The Book of Proverbs says, "The fear of the Lord is the beginning of wisdom." The Hebrew word that is translated, "fear" is more accurately translated; reverence. This reverence or honoring God will cast out all our fears and will set us free to truly be able to love God, love ourselves and to love one another. My fears can be paralyzing but this veneration of God truly sets me free. Many people avoid God because they think that it will imprison them with a set of cumbersome, repressive rules. It is in fact the opposite. Without God, we cannot be free. The word of God never says no to us without a better yes for us. You can't play "Hide and Seek" with God. You can't hide from God and then seek contentment; only God is our permanent contentment. There is no safe haven from God, but there is a safe haven in God. These medical missionary trips with "His Healing Hands" help me serve and administer to others and in return, God ministers to me and replaces my damaging pride with useful humility. Rules don't have the power to make us good. Only God can change us and give us a new loving nature.

"His Healing Hands"

"His Healing Hands," a medical humanitarian, missionary organization has enabled me to use my abilities in medicine, and teaching, and created an environment to allow me to exercise my desire to treat the poor and the abandoned segment of our world population. There is tremendous need in the world for caring individuals to share themselves with the downtrodden of humanity. We all can do something: we all can support; we all can encourage, and we all can contribute in some way to the underprivileged of civilization. "His Healing Hands" requires medical personnel, and certainly all organizations need money but our immediate need is compassionate, loving, and empathetic people of all talents and all ages and all persuasions. Although we are a Christian, faith based organization; there is no belief system requirement for accompanying us on our trips to help the poor and disadvantaged. Everyone needs help at some stage in his or her life, and to those of us that have been given much; much is expected. If we don't help others, who will? Sir Edmund Burke said, "All that is necessary for evil to triumph, is for good men to do nothing." We who can, must do something. The harvest is plentiful but the workers are few. There are many harassed and helpless people on the planet, and I considerate it an honor and a privilege to try to help them. My motivation relates to what God has done for me, but you may have a different incentive. My example is the sacrificial love of Jesus and I am grateful to Him, but I'm sure that you also have an example of the love of God that encourages you to help your fellow man, or the experience of others aiding you.

"His Healing Hands" is the framework whereby we can use our gifts to help the pitiable of the human race. We have many complex, intricate, multifaceted problems in the world today. As one little person, I cannot conceive of how I can help or aid in their solutions. It is very frustrating when I think of my own blessed life, my knowledge of God through the Bible and the rules or commandments that are written to bless me, not burden me, juxtaposed to the retched condition of the peoples of the world today: medically, politically, religiously, and in social and economic poverty. I believe that "His Healing Hands" can supply some of the answers to the world's dilemmas, and we: you and me can be part of the solution. I can treat one patient at a time and try to make that one person's life better. I can alleviate some of their pain and suffering, help their personal hygiene, provide warmth and clean water, and encourage one of them at a time. This may seem to be a "drop in the bucket," but when you think about it, it really is everything to that one person and to me. "His Healing Hands" can frame our gifts, and our humanity to an inhumane world living without the blessings of God. This organization has the contacts in six continents to help the poor. It arranges the team and supplies the different needed medicines for each country based on our past experiences of the different patient populations. It arranges the travel accommodations and the clinic sites. All and everyone are welcome. We all pay our own way and all donations are used for the patients that we treat. This organization can bridge the gap between all cultures, countries, religions, and political ideation because we will gladly treat anyone without regard to ethnicity. We consider all the peoples of the world to be God's people whether they recognize Him or not, because we recognize Him. We have been requested to go to countries that usually don't allow American aid or Christian aid because we will go anywhere and provide needed medical care as we have learned to become very mobile. Our logo is a pair of strong but helpful, gentle hands lifting up the entire world. This organization can and will grow in direct relationship to the helpful workers that are willing to join us. We are a non-denominational, non-sectarian, humanitarian, tax-exempt organization that has successfully treated and cared for tens of thousands of patients free of charge. We have developed a medical model that works and uplifts both the patients and the workers. We work very hard but we have a lot of enjoyment in this very rewarding endeavor. One of the motivations of mine to write this book is to present "His Healing Hands" organization to all peoples who either need our care or would like to take the opportunity to join us in giving something back to the peoples of the world that share our planet.

We would like to encourage and help local churches that want to create a missionary program with their members by availing themselves of our model. A short compact disc demonstrating how a church can set up missionary trips through "His Healing Hands," supporting their local members who become their own missionaries can be sent to any church group. The local church can support their own members with prayer and financial support while joining a "His Healing Hands" team.

We believe in the Fatherhood of God and the Brotherhood of Man. We understand that you can't love God if you don't love His creation. Our love for our fellow man has increased our ability to love God. No one has seen God but if God is love and we emulate His love, as He is, so we will become, and reflect His glory. We live in this very complex world with complicated, convoluted problems that have no easy answers, but we can aid one patient at a time and at least temporarily alleviate some degree of misery and anguish. We are not just humanitarian "talkers" but we are humanitarian "doers." We invite you to join in this Brotherhood of Man and leave this globe better than you found it, with the addition of your healing hands.

"His Healing Hands" has partnered with Global Aid Network (GAIN), Mission to the World, Campus Crusade for Christ (CCC), and Northwest Medical Teams. Our teams comprise at least one medical doctor, at least one pharmacist, several nurses, paramedical personnel, students interested in the medical field, encouragers, lay people to help with logistics and crowd control, anyone interested in helping the poor, and some of our children and their friends. Since the first several trips in nineteen hundred and ninety-nine, several of the young people joining us have been encouraged to enter the field of medicine; going to medical school, pharmacy school, and nursing school. Others have been encouraged to return to a college career. Many non-medical people have joined us and they have been a tremendous asset to our team and the patients. At first, they all question whether or not they will be able to help us help the patients because of their lack of medical training. However, these are the folks that are usually the busiest workers during our medical clinics. We usually have some of our people play instruments and we do daily morning devotionals and pray for the people of the country. These devotionals are always optional, but even non-believers have enjoyed this time together. We have taught many of the non-medical personnel to take blood pressure, test blood sugar, fit glasses, and help in the pharmacy with medicines under the direction of the pharmacist. Our teams have handed out supplies of food and clothing, helped to set up tents and aid in the creation of water filtration systems. Our organization has been stretched to provide more rapid relief and response to cities after major disasters. We have sent groups to

Indonesia after the tsunami, Pakistan after the earthquake, Guatemala and the Philippines after the mud-slides, and Mississippi after Hurricane Katrina.

Some of us have been honored by the local churches, who have allowed us to preach to their congregations, teach in their Sunday schools, and give our testimonies while showing the Jesus film set up by Campus Crusade for Christ. Every one of our trips has been beneficial to all the people that we have served, and we have been enthusiastically invited back to treat their people again. During each trip, we try to set aside some time in the country to get some rest and relaxation, enjoying the local customs, food, and sights. We have been: on a safari

in Africa, seen the Taj Mahal in India, spent time at the beaches of Vietnam, Thailand, Philippines, India, Belize, Zanzibar and Fiji, gone to the Forbidden City and the Great Wall in China, seen Count Dracula's Castle in Transylvania, Romania, and went sport fishing on Lake Tanganyika in Tanzania just to name a few outings. We have shopped around the world. My wife says our house looks like Pier One. We have hiked in the mountains of Pakistan, Guatemala and Peru. Some of our team have scuba dived and snorkeled in Fiji and Belize. Our young people have set up an amazing fire-works display on the fourth of July in China to demonstrate to the locals how we in the United States celebrate our independence and love of freedom. Sometimes in America, we tend to take our freedoms for granted but when you see peoples of the world risking their lives just to read a Bible, it becomes apparent why all these people admire what we are and what we possess. Freedom is not free. Many Americans paid a costly price to give us the freedoms we enjoy today. But the most exciting experiences of these trips are spending time with the peoples of different cultures of the world. There is nothing in this world to match the high emotion of knowing that you made a difference in someone's life and made it better. "His Healing Hands" invites all people from eight to eighty to join us on future adventures. I guarantee that it will transform your perspective and your outlook on

A lunch break with our team, including our families, and hosts in China.

life and your ability to appreciate living will be increased and changed forever. "His Healing Hands" has a web site, hishealinghands.com where anyone, anywhere in the world can see in advance our upcoming trips or e-mail questions to us or pray for our service to others or donate to our organization. We are also starting a Christian radio station that can be accessed, in the future, through this web site at hishealinghands.com and click on the radio button. Our office number is 805-434-3653, and our fax number is 805-434-1098. The poor and the downcast need you. Please help us help them.

"His Healing Hands," medical fair and clinic in Fresno, World Import Center.

"His Healing Hands", International Organization We Have Not Forgotten To Serve Our People At Home

Jesus told His disciples to go to the ends of the earth preaching and teaching the good news and healing every disease and illness. He also told them not to abandon their own people. "His Healing Hands" medical humanitarian organization has not forgotten about treating the poor, the needy, and the impoverished people of our own country. We have held clinics in our hometowns within a radius of fifty miles. We have performed physical examinations at summer camps outside of Los Angeles, California. We have held clinics in the inner cities of Fresno, California and the inner city of Los Angeles, California, and aided the people of Mississippi after the devastating Hurricane Katrina. We have held clinics in predominantly Hispanic areas of Santa Maria, California, and held medical fairs in many different cities. We have arranged for diabetic screening and high blood pressure screening in our local community through Community Medical Centers, serving the indigent California Medi-Cal population. We will gladly continue to serve the local communities, as the neighborhood governments will allow. Although it is obviously logistically easier to help in our own country, our own government makes it difficult for us to receive permission to treat American patients. After the New Orleans hurricane, our organization which is very mobile and flexible, volunteered to go to the devastated areas. The Health and Human Services Department of the United States told us they would call us if they needed us and they never called even after we inquired of them multiple times. We are still waiting for their call. We decided to work through a local church to help feed the hungry and cloth the poor, although we were not allowed to treat them medically in spite of our United States medical licenses. We will not allow our own government to deter us from our mission to treat the poor, the helpless and the needy. It seems to be a lot easier to treat the Mexican American population in our area.

We held a medical clinic in Santa Maria, California, on the central coast of California in a Mexican barrio. Most of our patients were illegal aliens whom the politically correct people call undocumented guest workers. These people don't receive adequate medical care because of their fear of any governmental employees reporting them to the authorities, including hospital workers. They also have a natural fear of hospitals because the hospitals that they are accustomed to in Mexico are places where you go to die, and once you are admitted, you don't walk out of the hospital on your own power. We examined these patients in a home where a local pastor was setting up a church in the midst of their barrio. These people came to our clinic because they trust this pastor. We screened these patients for hypertension and diabetes and a large percentage, above forty per cent, were positive for both without prior knowledge of these diseases. We gave them sample medicines and made arrangements to hold a clinic in this area on a routine monthly basis. We examined the women and children during the daylight hours and toward evening the men came to our clinics after they finished working in the strawberry fields. It was obvious that these were very hard workers, by the nature of their clothes stained with strawberries, their hair filled with dust, and their tired sunburned moistened faces. Illegal Mexican American workers are currently a hotbed issue in

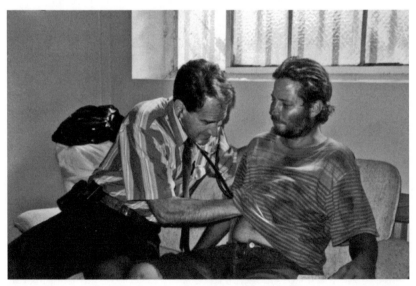

Here I am examining a homeless person in a "Mission to the World," Fresno, California Clinic.

California. But "His Healing Hands" is interested in helping the indigent without regard to any political issue, which is why we can bridge the gap between ethnic groups, political issues, religions, or socioeconomic status. We are not a governmental organization and our only agenda is to treat people created in God's image, and profess and demonstrate His love. These immigrants felt the love and understood our motivation and started to trust us as well. The best way to change minds about Americans is people to people contact and care.

We held a similar medical faire with screening examinations and blood tests in Fresno, California under the auspices of "World Impact." This is an organization that plants missionary families right in the middle of the inner city to live directly with the poor people in their own neighborhood. This population in Fresno is not made up of Mexican American families. They are poor white single parent families who are mainly alcoholics and drug abusers, with aids, hepatitis, and sexually transmitted diseases. Some people feel that the system has failed these American citizens and others feel that these people have failed America and our country of infinite opportunities and freedom. Again, we at "His Healing Hands" make no such value judgments or take sides in these types of debates. Our most prevalent feelings are compassion, empathy, and sympathy, with the mind-set of "there but for the grace of God go I." These sad people get severe infections as a result their low resistance due to their underlying chronic diseases. They also have a high incidence of mental disorders, which makes them more difficult to treat and to comply with our instructions. We also have to be careful not to give them medicines that they will turn around and sell on the streets for their next fix. As you can see, we run the gamut of medical problems and social ills, making our clinics anything but boring. The most needy and the saddest group that we treat are the children brought in by these homeless, socially outcast parents. These children did not choose this type of life, as many of their parents prefer.

Poor, underfed, needy children can break your heart, whether they are in Tanzania, Africa or Fresno, California. The missionaries of "Mission to the World," living in the midst of these people are able to gain their trust and thereby make a difference in their lives. We have brought our children to many of the underprivileged ghettos of the world but these missionary families permanently live amongst the people they are trying to help, with their children going to their schools, sharing their playgrounds, and living on the same streets. The people learn to trust these missionaries and the missionaries in turn learn to trust God with their most prized possessions; their children. Many of these families that they try to help are homeless: living on the streets or in cars, or in homeless shelters.

We have treated the homeless in these shelters and I have spent the night as a chaperone in these shelters. The circumstances of these people are not what you might expect. Many of the fathers work during the day, the children go to the local schools, and the mothers roam the streets with younger children and spend their time in the parks, only to return to the shelters at night for a meal and a bed. Many Americans are one paycheck away from this scenario. This state of affairs for many of our citizens has repeated itself all across our country in all of the major cities. These working homeless fall through the cracks of our social service safety net since they make too much money for assistance but not enough to pay for an apartment to rent. We must improve our educational institutions to help train these people for gainful employment with a living wage commensurate with the state of our economy and the cost of living the American dream. Again. "His Healing Hands" tries to fill the gap now, until our learning institutions and our social service system and our humanitarian organizations can permanently help these unfortunate people. Those of us that have a lot must share with those that have little, not out of guilt but out of gratefulness to God. Having been brought up on the streets of New York City amidst poverty, I can easily identify with these people. I personally believe that we as American's have an obligation to help these people help themselves. We must lend a helping hand to these people without creating dependency or making them a permanent ward of the state.

I remember as a teenager trying to climb over a fence of a closed playground after hours and falling about ten feet to the pavement and landing awkwardly on my left leg. I was unable to bear weight on my foot and my friends with laughter carried me to the emergency room at Bellevue Hospital on the east side of New York City. They treated me even though I was a minor. They took an x-ray of my fractured leg and then set it in a cast. No one asked for my insurance, as medical insurance didn't exist in the fifties. No one called my mother for permission, as none was required. And no one asked me for money that they knew I didn't have. It was a simpler time with simpler solutions. It was all about helping the needy and getting the job done. It also created a feeling of gratefulness in my heart with a desire to give back to society when I was in a position to help others as they had helped me.

As a fourth year medical student at Albert Einstein Medical School in New York City in nineteen sixty-eight, I worked in an emergency room in Lincoln Hospital in the south Bronx. It was a converted bread factory and the facilities were woefully inadequate. We served a large black and Puerto Rican population with many warring gangs. It was used as a backdrop in the film, "Fort Apache, the South Bronx," starring Paul Newman. We had to park our vehicles in a parking lot next to the hospital with a paid guard protecting our cars and escorting us from the emergency room to our cars. We couldn't leave the hospital at night, as it was too dangerous. One day our ride sharing automobile wouldn't start. The guard told us that the battery was stolen, but for five dollars he could get it back. We returned to the hospital, gave him ten minutes and when we returned, our same battery was back and hooked up properly. Our own security guard had stolen our battery and shook us down for five dollars. Another time, I was assisting in an operation on a stabbed gang member and the rival gang stormed the operating room and finished off the job and the patient died. Although this was a crazy place to work, as a fourth year medical student, I was allowed to perform many procedures in the emergency room when the "real" doctors were overwhelmed by acute life threatening emergencies. This emergency room was so busy that the non- life threatening gunshot wounds waited in the hallway, with blood soaked wrappings, while we took care of the bleeding stab wounds. The experienced nurses helped me and when I pleaded that I had never done this type of procedure before, they said, "Doctor, you are all we've got." My anxiety was high but my experiences were great. I loved the action and the excitement of the inner city even though it was the result of vengeful, ruthless behavior. I wasn't a believer at that time but I now understand that even then, God was preparing me for medical missionary work in future similar circumstances. When I discuss by beliefs with inner city poor people, I can relate to them and hopefully they can relate to me. God has used some of my negative experiences for His positive outcomes. I truly believe this is God's providential care and preparation, and I know it is miraculous in nature. Sometimes in our routine mundane daily actions, we don't recognize God's hand in our lives, but reflection and hindsight are great teachers.

Four nurses and two medical assistants in front of their
ambulance (truck) in Baja, Mexico

Another one of our local ministries is in Baja California, two hours
south of the United States border at San Diego, California. We have a
very large Mexican American population in California who have many
relatives in Mexico, and as a result of our Mexican patient population,
most of us can speak Spanish. We have traveled to San Vincente, Baja
California to hold medical clinics, through their social service medical
organization, to treat patients in their clinics and labor camps. These
camps have large populations with many mothers and infants who have
been bussed up from southern Mexico to work in the fields (the campo),
for six dollars per day, which is much more money than these laborers
can make at home. They work very hard under backbreaking conditions
in the hot fields, with their babies on their backs. They all have aches
and pains, infections, and gastritis from the new type of foods that they
are supplied by the company store. Their babies get a lot of upper respiratory infections. It is very rewarding to treat these people because
they have very easily treatable diseases, which only require a little care,
medicines, and simple medical counseling. I love to treat these grateful
hard working people. Instead of driving eight hours from our central
California homes, at times we have had pilots from the "Flying Samaritans" fly us in their small planes to a little private narrow dirt airstrip

Boys in a Baja labor camp, cling to the
soccer ball that we gave to them

in the neighboring town of San Quinten. On one of these trips, which
was medically very fruitful, we needed God to directly intervene on our
return flight home.

It was on a Sunday, and we had just finished a morning clinic.
We needed to get home because all of us had busy patient schedules
in our offices on Monday morning back in California. I am not a pilot,

Short makeshift rock runway in Baja, California.
The one engine plane in the foreground had to lift
up off the road quickly

and I didn't realize that when you fly in small planes, you can't have the mind-set of being in a hurry. The weather looked clear and we took off from our narrow short rock runway without a hitch. We headed to the coastline and followed it north to Ensenada, where we had to go through customs. The wind started to increase but we landed in Ensenada without incident. We checked the forecast and it said a storm was approaching from the west over the Pacific Ocean. We discussed staying in Ensenada over night but we were all anxious to get home so we wouldn't miss our office patients on Monday. We took off but the storm approached rapidly and our pilot was not instrument rated, so we returned to Ensenada Airport. Our copilot was instrument rated and she said that we could fly over the mountains toward the East and avoid the brunt of the storm. We all wanted to get home and we decided that it was worth the risk. We were in a single engine plane; flying and risks do not go together. We took off again at the coast, which was cloudy but clear, and headed up and over the mountains. We were gaining altitude when the storm hit. I have no knowledge of flying but the weather and the pilot's discussions seemed ominous. The plane was lurching upward and the pilots were talking to each other in a very nervous talkative manner as if to reassure themselves. I heard the pilot say that we were at maximum power and maximum climbing attitude. We were flying on instruments since our visibility was zero. We were not able to contact Tijuana Airport on the radio. We were in a radio dead space. At the time, I didn't know about icing on the wings but I later learned that this was a very dangerous situation. The wings outside which I got a glimpse of, off and on, were starting to accumulate ice. I later told this story to my friend Rod, who was an experienced pilot. He told me that the combination of maximum power and attitude, with ice on the wings, making the plane heavier over mountains, with no visual aids or radar and no radio communication, was disastrous. The plane shook and we continued to climb at maximum power and lift for twenty minutes. When we broke through the fog, clouds and weather, we were only several hundred feet above the mountains. When the pilots clapped their hands in jubilation, I then knew we had been in trouble and then I became frightened. God had surely lifted that underpowered plane up and over the mountains to clear skies. We were above the weather but we were lost and couldn't find the nearest airport. We were over Mexicali Airport and the border patrol planes had to scramble and came up to lead us to the airport runway. When we landed and were safely in the small terminal, all the other pilots asked if we had just arrived in that single engine plane and nervously laughed when we said yes. We were imprudent and made a lot of foolhardy decisions but God saved us from ourselves. Looking back at our careless judgments, I realized that we had never prayed or asked God to help us with our decision. In my many years as a believer and walking with the Lord, I have come to understand some of the extent of my sinful pride, and my not including God in my daily life. They say there are no atheists in foxholes, but where is our daily, routine, everyday commitment to the Lord of the universe? Dwight Moody, a great evangelist was challenged by the statement, "The world has yet to see, what God can do through one man entirely committed to Him." Moody led thousands of people to the Lord during his lifetime, but certainly there has never been a totally committed man to God, except for Jesus, who was God. I want to be a committed man to God and be used by Him; I am still trying to approach that goal and I will never stop trying. I told my "airplane near miss story" to my friend Rod, an experienced pilot and instructor and he shook his head and said the pilots should never have taken off and that they made repeated cardinal mistakes.

This friend Rod, who flew helicopters into battle in Vietnam, related a story to me about how God had directly spoken to him in a similar frightening experience, when he was nineteen years old flying search and rescue helicopter missions in Vietnam. Rod was a Warrant Officer One in Lane Heliport in Onson, Vietnam west of Quinh Seaport in nineteen seventy. He flew thousands of rescue missions and his helicopter was repeatedly shot at by antiaircraft fire. The most dangerous part of the missions were approaching and leaving the pickup zones and being caught on the ground for any length of time. On one of these missions in August, Rod's helicopter crew was assigned to pick up and move a battalion commander and his aid in the field, take off and orbit the area and take the commander to another remote outpost. They took off from the base and made a high overhead approach to the pickup zone. This meant that they flew at three thousand feet at full speed as if they were going past the drop area and the suddenly spiral or corkscrew down to the pickup point. Rod reports that this camouflage technique rarely worked and it didn't work this time either. Rod had the controls and as he spiraled the helicopter down, he heard the sound of rapid staccato popcorn bursts. He turned to ask his crew chief about the sound and saw holes appear in the floor of his UH-1 (Huey) helicopter and aluminum pieces flying all around him. Two antiaircraft rounds blew out his chin bubble at his feet (Plexiglas at the pilots feet). One bullet creased the other pilot's helmet, and the second bullet went up Rods' pant leg and exited out his shirt and lodged inside his armored seat. Rod patted himself down and discovered to his amazement that he wasn't hit. He brushed off the Plexiglas that exploded onto his face because he couldn't see and the other pilot yelled, "I got it, I got it," and took the controls. They dove for the cover of trees and flew at top speed to about three kilometers away. They assessed the damage, which was a lot of bullets and debris, but they were still flying with all the dials, the fluids and the pressure reflecting normal engine conditions. All the crew members examined themselves for injuries and only one of the crew had a graze of his third web space of his right hand. They decided to turn back, finish the mission and return to pick up the captain and his aid. They radioed the base on the ground and told the captain that he and his aid had ten seconds after they landed to get on board and then they were going to take off with or without them. Rod again had the controls and for the first time he realized that in one minute he might be dead. "I was nineteen years old and I thought that this may be it. I quietly prayed to the Lord and asked Him to be with me." Rod is six foot-three in height and weighs two hundred and twenty pounds and at age twenty was very physically fit. Even today, he is a very strong and active fearless vigorous man who is a retired fire-captain, who races sports cars. At times, the bravest of us will be scared. He states that after his short prayer, "I immediately felt a presence and a creepy feeling of someone staring at me from behind. I thought it was one of my crew-members but as I turned no one was staring at me and I heard a strange voice. It was a different type of voice. It went through my brain and it was not over the intercom of my headset." Rod related to me that he was brought up in a Dutch reformed Church and just before he left for Vietnam, he made a profession of faith. He said that he thought the five-minute prayers that the pastor prayed in church always seemed very long to him. "In Vietnam I prayed at night before going to bed and after I finished I would look at my watch and forty-five minutes had gone by." Rod is not a man to jump to conclusions, hear voices or hallucinate out of fear. "This voice I heard had a different quality than any human voice I had ever heard. It said, 'everything is going to be all right. I'm here with you.' I instantly had a calm feeling overtake me and I knew that it was the voice of an Angel of the Lord. We flew in at tree-top level and dropped to the landing zone, hovering three feet above the ground, ready to land. Both the captain and his aid dove into the helicopter before we could land and we went to full power until we got five kilometers south and at a safe elevation. I heard the voice again; saying, 'I have to go now, I'm needed elsewhere.' I felt the presence leave me and it went through the roof of the helicopter." Rod told me that he didn't tell anyone about this occurrence for fifteen years as he thought, "I didn't want anyone to think that I was wacko." He told his mother about this episode over five years later, and she was sure that it had happened and that God had protected her son as a result of her prayers. I first heard Rod's story, in a Bible class that I was teaching. We were discussing whether angels were real. Rod raised his hand and told us about his personal communication with an angel of the Lord. Rod said, "There is no doubt in my mind that God is real and angels are real; I know it." He told me that after going through this near death experience, everything in life seemed more alive and vibrant. "Reds were redder, food was tastier, and relationships were more intense." In escaping death, life became more significant.

God is a God of miracles, a God of protection, and a God of loving kindness. To those committed to Him, He is also a God of provision, and for those who don't know Him, He is a God wanting to provide His Son, who is offered as a free gift to anyone who will accept Him. "His Healing Hands" wants to reflect this love and care on a one to one basis to all humanity around the world and in our own neighborhood. There are many stories of God's protection and provision and many people know and feel the truth of the existence of a real knowable God.

LANDING OF THE JEWS AT
SHINGLY (CRANGANORE) IN 72 C.E.

The Old Testament Scrolls in a Synagogue in Shingly,
India established after the burning of Jerusalem

Can You Handle
The Truth?

In a recent courtroom scene in a popular movie, a witness on the stand yells out "you can't handle the truth." This was in response to a demand from the defense for the factual reality concerning the trial. God offers us the truth about ourselves and the world that He created. But the question remains; can we handle and act on this truth? Can we look into the mirror and admit to the truth of what we see?

I have traveled all around the world and I have come to understand that the majority of the peoples of the globe are very religious. This spirituality, however, doesn't include piety or holiness. These religions have names, they have liturgies, they include prayers, and rules and regulations that are required to please their leaders and "a higher power." They have demands, but these burdens are loose and hassle free. They enable us to answer the question, "what religion do you follow?" without life changing obligations. They facilitate tax-free donations and allow us to alleviate some guilt feelings. They are like an easy listening radio station or music in an elevator or dentist office, supplying background noise without thought. Do they offer the truth and is that truth relativistic? Can it be different for everyone? Truth by definition is true and cannot be changed to accommodate our needs, feelings, or desires. It is very dogmatic by designation and design. Can we handle the truth? However you might ask, what is the truth and where can I find it? Like you, I have looked for the truth all my life, and when I read the Bible, I am looking into that mirror where the truth leaps out at me. When we read The Word, it is a mirror that teaches us understanding of ourselves and our strengths and shortcomings. This Word, when applied to our lives leads us to live differently. When we look into a mirror, we proceed to improve our appearance. We comb our hair, clean our face, and view the changed result. We need to do the same, with our attitudes, our desires, our speech, and our actions, and then we need to scrutinize the altered outcome. This mirror, the Bible, doesn't teach guilt but it teaches gratefulness to our Savior. He is also our example and we should desire to imitate His righteousness that is truth.

Previously, I have outlined why I believe that the Bible is our manual for life and salvation and that Jesus is the truth and the life. Christianity is not a religion but a relationship with the Christ: the Messiah, the Redeemer. We have more manuscripts of the Bible than any other literature of antiquity. It is written in four different languages by forty different authors over two thousand years and yet, it is consistent without contradictions from the beginning to the end. One-fourth of the Bible is predictive prophecy and many of the prophetic declarations have occurred just as they were predicted. Never has a Bible prediction been wrong and extra biblical literature, history, and archeological finds have proven it to be accurate, time and time again. The Bible's advise for living is sound and has been confirmed by every generation. The principles of the Bible, work for both nations and individuals. If we look around the world today, it is obvious that the wealthiest, most powerful, and most socially successful nations in the world starting with the United States are Judeo-Christian based nations. The poorest nations of the world are Moslem based nations in spite of the oil rich leaders. I know this because those are the nations that "His Healing Hands" usually tries to help with our medical humanitarian aid. The Bible works. It invented marriage between a man and a woman. This allows for a strong family unit that procreates and populates the planet. The rules for individuals and families are meant to protect these vital institutions. The Bible teaches fidelity, socially acceptable behavior, governmental regulations, and legal and medical principles, and they all benefit humanity. Contrary to public opinion, the Bible is very scientific, knowing that the sun was bigger than the moon during the time of moon worshipping. It described and predicted the major civilizations and it's rulers even before they arose. The Bible stated that the planet was round well before Columbus came to the New World. The Bible answers the complicated profound questions of life with very simple, straightforward, self- evident answers. It is the most published and read book on record. The Bible is a literary masterpiece and the most quoted book in the world. The Bible is truly a manual for living and knowing God. If you read it with an open non-judgmental mind, I believe you will come to the same conclusions. Everyone owes it to themselves to at least read it and experience its wisdom. The Bible states in no uncertain terms that Jesus is our Creator God.

Jesus claimed to be God in the flesh and this assertion was backed up by miracles, eyewitnesses, and history. After His crucifixion followed by His resurrection, He appeared to over five hundred eyewitnesses. For the past two thousand years, the truth of Jesus has been challenged even up to this very day. Books and movies such as "The Last Temptation Of Christ" and "The DaVinci Code" have desperately tried to dispel the truth of Jesus and have failed miserably. His believers have been martyred and ridiculed and yet, Christianity is still growing all over the world, including places where it is unlawful to even have a Bible. Truth cannot be stopped and God's plan will succeed. But can we handle its truth and not only know the truth but live by this truth?

Unlike the other "religions," Christian faith does stipulate actions and makes demands on its followers. We are to feed the hungry, cloth the naked, comfort the sick, and share with the poor. The Bible says faith without works is a dead faith. Christianity in its relationship to Christ is a living, caring, sharing, active belief. Its truth gets results because it is alive with good deeds prepared by God for us to accomplish. God does not want our rituals or our sacrifices or our declarations of faith, if they are not accompanied by our spiritual service of worship, which is our very lives, all and every part of us. That is the truth. Can I, can you, handle it?

The truth that we cannot handle is the truth about ourselves, not the truth about God. The debate between creationists and evolutionists is not about the existence of an all-powerful Creator God. That argument is a smokescreen to hide the truth about us: about me, about you. The Bible as a mirror convicts us about ourselves, but if we are open to its truth, it will convert us to the truth. The new combination of words, "relativistic truth," meaning the truth is different based on different circumstances, situations and individual interpreters, is a contradiction of terminology, and understanding. It negates all truth so we can be in control of our lives. It is all about control, not wanting anyone especially an all-powerful God to run our lives. When we realize that God created all of us and He is ultimately in control, we release our false pride, and the truth becomes apparent. We think what we are, but we become what we think. I have an impression of myself but without the objectivity of a separate guidebook, my life will become my own fantasy. Most people complain that they are not photogenic and "that picture of me doesn't look like me," or "that's my bad side," or "I take a horrible picture." Outwardly and inwardly we have a false impression of ourselves. The camera doesn't lie and it reflects reality. The Bible is a mirror, and its truth is Gods truth before our eyes. This truth will set us free, but again; can we handle the truth?

I have stated before that I have trained myself to learn from the negative as well as the positive. This is actually a very Jewish characteristic as it is used extensively in the Old Testament especially in the book of Psalms and in the book of Proverbs. During my first missionary trip to Haiti, it seems that everything about that country was negative, and this relates back to the results of the opposite of truth; namely falsehood or theologically speaking, sin. Haiti is an example of hatred of God, abhorrence of whites, total depravity, selfishness, exultation of sin and Devil worship.

In the late nineteenth century, when the white slave masters were brutally subjugating the African, black slave population, a group of slaves made a union with the devil. They prayed to the devil that they would follow him and dedicate the country to him, if he helped them kill and overtake their white slave masters and their white God. They sealed this covenant in blood. They killed animals and white slave masters and drank their blood in a ceremony of devil worship. A few of the black slaves escaped to the mountains and would come down at night and one by one kill a white slaver and capture his rifle. They went back into the mountains and sharpshooters would pick off a white slave boss in the fields and set blacks free to hide in the mountains while obtaining another rifle. Little by little they reduced the white slaver population and by guerilla warfare were able to take over the country and set the slave population free. Voodoo became the national religion; dictatorship has been the predominant governmental institution with anarchy and brutality the prevailing form of national societal organization. This godless country doesn't work for the people. They have no family units, no love of God or their fellow man, no sense of right and wrong, and no absolute truth to guide them. The opposite of trusting and obeying God creates a disaster. Haiti is considered the poorest country in the Americas, where everyone tries to escape even at the cost of risking their life. If you are hateful, you will exhibit hate. If you love, you will exude love. Obedience to the God of the Bible is the only way to demonstrate true love. An unloving, godless people in an unloving, godless country will never work because we are created by God with some of His attributes, which will never translate into godless success. Everyone needs God and He will bless us if we acknowledge Him. Even atheists, who deny God are benefiting from living under god invented principles and institutions. Our families, our government with its system of checks and balance based on the sin nature of man, and our desire to help each other all come from godly biblical principles. Our definition of good verses evil comes from God, and all expressions of love come from God.

The good news about Haiti is that there are missionaries who love God and they know that God will never abandon them or the people of Haiti. God loves all people whom He created. When the people of Haiti come to a knowledge of Jesus, their Lord and Savior, the truth will set them free.

Conclusion / Beginnings

So, what have I learned from my medical missionary trips and my "deal" with God? I saw first hand that God is always faithful and righteous and loving and just and forever upholds His covenant. He is a covenant keeping God. In fact, He even upholds my side of the bargain as He did with Abraham, when God told him that He would be his shield and his great reward. Has my faith increased? Yes it has, but I have learned that it is a process that contains many parts, and not a simple case of my "grand" faith to make me a bold witness for God. It entails prayer directly to God the Father that Jesus prepared for us by sacrificing Himself for our sins. It involves righteousness, which means obedience to God's righteousness. It contains love of God and one another, which is the mark of a believer in this world. If we apply this love to others, it will result in forgiveness of others as God has forgiven us. It means understanding God's providence and that He prepares the way for

The Western Wall in the Old City of Jerusalem, where prayers are written on papers and stuffed in the old wall. Where is your hope?

us to walk in His light. It is surrounded by the fellowship of believers with different spiritual gifts whose whole is greater than the sum of its parts. This involves knowing our gift, using this gift in the advancement of God's Kingdom, and being good stewards of our gifts. It is understanding that God is our portion, our gift from Him and our ultimate reward.

Jesus is our sacrificial Lamb of God that not only takes away the sins of the world, but also allows us to have loving fellowship with each other. During my entire life, the newspapers have been filled with reports of war, atrocities, murder, and hate related crimes, demonstrating man's inhumanity to man. The violence in the Middle East is an example of our inhumanity and our inability to solve our own problems. These tribulations are the result of our sinfulness and our sinful nature. Only God can create peace in the Middle East, and He will. In my medical missionary travels with "His Healing Hands," I have directly observed evidence of man's brutality to one another. I never have to view another horror film. Without God, man has made a horror of history. Viewed as a simple mathematical equation: my sin + your sin = our sin. God's love for us, confirmed by giving His only begotten Son as a loving sacrifice, has not only paved our way to heaven, but has given us an example of unconditional sacrificial love, that can be the salvation of humanity. This can be displayed in another equation: my sin − my sin erased by the sacrifice of Jesus' death + your sin − your sin erased by Jesus' substitutionary atonement = righteousness and forgiveness. Christians are called to be in the world but not of the world, and to be transformed by God and not to be conformed to the world system and the world view. The world's values, its pleasures, and its desires are frequently at odds with the righteousness and the love of God.

As a Christian, who tries to follow biblical principles in my life, interacting with people and trying not to be affected by the values of the world is a daily difficult endeavor. It is not a theoretical discussion; it is a very practical day-by-day exercise in living. Recently, I was considering a partnership with a very helpful, loving, caring individual who is a nonbeliever. I had a decision to make and I was bothered in my soul regarding its biblical outcome. I prayed about the decision, I consulted the Bible, and then I went to my best friend Bob, who I knew would give me wise Christian council. Bob is a wonderful godly man who walks closely with God while dealing with many worldly personalities in his work. His knowledge is from the Bible, which gives him a simple practical wisdom that is tempered with kindness and humility. My problem stemmed from a good idea and great business opportunity, which would bless many people including my family, my friends, the public, and indirectly our medical humanitarian organization, "His Healing Hands." However, and your ears must perk up and your eyes must open wide when you hear the word, however; if I went into partnership with a non-believer, the Bible says I would be unequally yoked. Picture an unmatched pair of oxen pulling with different strengths and different directions. It could be a disaster waiting to happen to the oxen, the cart and all its passengers. This is not to imply that, as a Christian, I am any better then my potential partner. It only implies a potential unmatched relationship doomed from the start. I needed to be in the world but not affected by its values. The non-believing world can influence a believer and put pressure on a believer to conform to its worldly principles. I love Bruce's idea and I love and respect this future partner but this relationship would be a risk for me if it was unbiblical and ungodly. I went to Bob for advice, expecting a yea or a nay. His advice was better than a simple positive or negative response.

He also knows and likes Bruce and in fact, Bob introduced Bruce to me. Bob said, "It all depends on your relationship to God and not your relationship to Bruce." It is true that we are not to be unequally yoked and influenced by a world-view, and at the same time maintain our position in the world not to be conformed to it and to be a light for the unsaved. This tightrope walk can become a reality if we have a close, personal, intimate, reliant, dependent relationship to God, His Word, and His people, while immersed in prayer. Bobs' council is correct. The answer depends on my relationship to God and not my relationship to Bruce or anyone else. There are opportunities in life that may offer a significant gain. Bob's advice tells me that gain is not always godliness, but I know that godliness is always gain. I thank God for humble, wise men like Bob walking with the Lord, knowledgeable in the Word, and willing to give sound loving biblical advise. I must remain on guard but God will provide the armor for my defense and I have the opportunity to be a witness to Bruce as a committed believer whose deeds match my words. That is the key to being believable. I must not only read the Bible but I must live it.

History is usually written by outlining civilizations that rise and fall based on war and conquest; not love, truth and righteousness. We tend to think of war as the opposite of peace but peace follows war. War is man's way but peace is God's way when the swords and spears of man are hammered into the plowshares and pruning hooks of God. The world can be conquered if the love of God fills us and the will of God motivates us.

That combination cannot be stopped and the damaging world-view can be overcome if the word of God lives in us. The Belgian nuns at Mother Teresa's "Home for the Destitute Dying" show how humanity can reverse its inhumanity, but this is such a rare example of sacrificial love that it amazes us, and makes us feel guilty and inadequate by its paradigm. I believe our world-view has changed in the last forty years to the point where we have accepted the mediocre instead of the best, the average instead of the superlative, and the ordinary instead of the exceptional. When I was in the army, I was given the second highest medal, after the Congressional Medal of Honor, for just doing what I was asked to do in an average way.

I was scheduled to be deployed to Vietnam in nineteen seventy-two, when my orders were mysteriously changed without my request, to an induction center in Los Angeles. This was a very boring job for a doctor recently out of a high-powered residency in surgery, so I decided to make the best of the situation. I did the job that I was asked to do and I did it correctly and efficiently, because it was really not a very demanding situation. Apparently, the Armed Forces at that time was not accustomed to anyone doing even the simplest job description correctly. They were impressed, made me a major and gave me the Joint Service Commendation. At the time, it didn't mean a lot to me, but now I'm glad it represents the fact that I did the job to the best of my ability. I would really like to get the Joint Service Commendation from God the Father, God the Son, and God the Holy Spirit. The Bible tells us to do the best we can in all things and do it unto God, as if He was our chief supervisor.

Sections of the Bible are over four thousand years old, and it is frequently asked how this old manuscript can possibly be applicable to my life in the twenty-first century? This is the wrong question or at least couched in an erroneous way. Wrong assumptions will always lead to incorrect conclusions. I ask you the reader, "How can it not be applicable when it is the manual inspired by the manufacturer?" If your Chevy breaks down or needs a new part, you consult the manual written by General Motors. We were created by God and at times, many times, we stray from the helpful advice of our Creator; the Manufacturer. When this happens and our lives don't run smoothly and we become a danger to ourselves and to others on the road of life, we need to consult the owner's manual. When your watch breaks, what better person to consult than the watchmaker? His advice will always be correct since he made every part of the watch and put it together. He knows how it ticks. Everything he says or does will be applicable to the watch, even a very old watch since it was fashioned by him from start to finish. We have been fashioned by the one and only Creator God and in His love, mercy, and grace; He has given us an owner's manual that never fails and is always appropriate, valid and germane to our lives. He has done it all for us and has had it all written down. I would guess that you have one of these manuals around your house collecting dust and waiting to be of service to you. You may even think that you don't conduct your life in any way related to the Bible. You might be surprised that most of our western values and even our words were first written in this Book. Everything in this world that works and stands up to the test of time is biblical, and it only works because it is consistent with the manual and its Creator. You can't get very far down the road of life if you put diesel fuel in a gas driven automobile or expect your watch to tell accurate time if you go swimming in the sea of life with a non-waterproof watch. Maybe, just maybe, you have been misled or not been made aware of the simplicity and the straightforwardness, and the ease of life when it is predicated on the correct manual. The wisdom of the Bible makes the simple eager open-minded people wise and reveals the people who are wise in their own minds to be simply unwise. God has done it all for us because of his immeasurable love for His most important creation. Everything that God created, He looked at it and said, "It is good." After creating man and woman, even you, He said, "It is very good."

I have been looking to develop more faith and I have learned about some of the ways to exercise the faith given to me by God. This process to obtain more faith is also displayed in God's miracles that He reveals to us but we must recognize these miracles as coming from God, and not rationalize them away to fit into our unbelievable and unscientific explanations. We must understand that our relationship with God is a very intimate relationship. We can speak directly to God the Father through Jesus the Son and we have God the Holy Spirit within us. This makes for the most intimate relationship that is possible. It appears to me that many believers don't allow themselves to benefit from this wonderful intimacy. This intimacy of being a child of God is what makes relationships between husbands and wives, parents and children, and friendships possible. We are created in the image of God, and when our actions and behavior reflect God's likeness, we are acting in a manner consistent with our creation. However, when we act apart from God's character, which the Bible calls sin, we are acting in a divergent manner from our original created purpose. We have exchanged the image of God for an image of a brutal creature. The Word of God states that we are created, "a little lower than the angels." It doesn't say that we are created a little higher than the beasts. Environmentalists and conservationists would have society believe that we are simply a different form of beast in the animal kingdom. But we are made in God's image with some of His attributes. We go to great length to save spotted owls and kit foxes at the detriment to humans, and allow millions of human babies to be sacrificed for inconvenience.

The elements of this process of obtaining more faith must be combined and covered with practical, active, demonstrable love and experienced and applied to others. Light will dispel darkness but it won't warm the earth without love. To walk in faith, means to walk in God's love, God's righteousness, and God's truth and if we rely on God for this walk, we will forget about ourselves and focus on God, who will increase our faith. My personal quest to serve God and acquire more faith has changed to a mission far beyond my personal walk and personal needs. It has completely changed from my plan to God's plan. Maybe this means that I am on the right tract because it is not a question of my faith but the faithfulness of God. It is not my peace but the peace of God. It is not a case of my joy but the joy of Jesus. Relying on my faith, or my peace, or my joy would depend on different circumstances and would therefore, vacillate and fluctuate. Our lives are frail and fleeting like a puff of smoke. But God never changes and is always the same, yesterday, today, and tomorrow. God is forever reliable and I am not. God can be fully trusted and I cannot be fully trusted. God can't lie and I am very capable of many lies. When I look back at my life, I see many hinge points or turning points, but there was one pivotal moment that everything in my life proceeding it has led up to, and everything passed that point has depended on. A hinge separates two sticks that come and go in different directions. My life was headed in a self-serving direction, and then I was presented with the inescapable truth, love, and righteousness of Jesus. The truth is that Jesus as God took the form of man and lived a sinless life and died as the substitution for my sins, and now has returned to the Father where He is an advocate for me. If this sounds personal and intimate, it is because faith in God is the most personal relationship that can ever exist. The love is a sacrificial love to take my place because the wages of sin is death, which we all deserve. The righteousness is the moral compass whereby we try and yearn to obey God based on the Word of God. God's truth allows us to have a yardstick, a plum bob, and a compass to guide our lives in an honest relationship with God and one another. His love allows us to love Him in return and love each other. His righteousness allows us to live moral lives and to treat each other with the respect that we want for ourselves. God is love. God is light. God is spirit. God is not A Spirit or A Light or A Lover. He is Spirit, He is Light, and He is Love. He is the definition of love, light and spirit. In a twinkling of an eye my life and path was changed from a self-serving life to a life of trying to serve my Creator God, who created me, loves me and died for me, so I could be with Him eternally. After that pivotal day of decision, the direction of my life was as far as East is from West. All I had to do was turn around on that axis but the change of direction heads me toward an eternal path toward Him. This is my testimony based on what I have seen and heard. I'm sure that you have your own testimony and I pray that it also involves, the one and only Creator God with resultant eternal life with God in time without end.

I had many unanswered questions in my life, until I approached this turning point and decided that Jesus of Nazareth was fully man while on earth and that He came from the Father, as he was fully God and became flesh and dwelt among us. This was God's plan throughout the Old and the New Testament. Before this pivotal point in my life that I can call an epiphany from God, I had all these complicated, deeply philosophical questions and problems. Now the answers are really very simple and at the same time very profound. We are to love as God loves. We are to believe in the truth of Jesus. We are to try to conduct ourselves with the righteousness of God. God says it, He does it, and I believe it. It's as simple and sound as that.

There is the Old Testament story of Abraham and Isaac climbing Mount Moriah to sacrifice to God. Isaac asked the most simple but profound question in the entire Bible. And Abraham answered with the simplest most profound answer in the entire Bible. As they climbed the mountain, Isaac asked, "Father, where is the lamb for the sacrifice?" Abraham answered, "God will provide for Himself the lamb." Years later in the Jordan River, John said, "Behold the lamb of God that takes away the sins of the world." God has provided the voluntary substitutionary sacrifice for you, if you choose to accept it. I respectfully pray that you choose the path of life.

A view of the Mount of Olives as seen from within
the Old City walls of Jerusalem.
Jesus said He will return in the same way He left
from the Mount of Olives.

"My Grace is Sufficient for Thee" - Epilogue

When I started to write this book, I talked about a "deal" that I made with God, and I said that I didn't want to be arrogant; but I was arrogant. A deal was never necessary because God's grace to the entire world and to me has always been sufficient and complete.

As long as I have been a believer, I have heard the term "to grow in God's grace," but I never understood it. This unmerited favor that God bestows on me through the completed work of Jesus has always been sufficient but I have to grow in its grace. Nothing can ever be added to the finished work of our Lord and Savior, Jesus Christ. It is whole, comprehensive, inclusive, absolute, total, and available to everyone. My faith in Him has been given to me freely, without the need of adding to it; but will I avail myself of this wonderful free gift? Since I accepted Jesus as my Lord and Savior, my attitudes and therefore, my entire outlook on life has changed. I am secure in what I believe. I am guided by the Word of God, and by the Holy Spirit in me. I can go directly to God in prayer with the assurance that He will answer me. I am certain of this based on my past experiences and past answered prayers, past fulfilled biblical prophecies, historical and archeological evidence, biblical eye witness accounts, and the undeniable evidence in my observation of the world and its miraculous creation. When you are sick, you want a medical doctor: not a medical textbook. When you are sued, you want a lawyer and not a legal treatise. And when you are dying and facing death, you want a Savior, not a doctrinal statement. If your hope for eternity is not God, what is it? Tell me of your hope. Where will you be? What will you think? Who will you know? Jesus is and was and always will be a real person and our Creator God. He offers everyone the free gift of eternal life with Him. I will forever pray on a daily basis that anyone who reads this book will find peace, love and joy in Jesus; everyone's Lord and Savior. My final statement is a prayer for all believers including myself. May we continue to grow in God's grace: Amen.

Contact His Healing Hands at:
- www.hishealinghands.com
  - Phone 805-434-3653
  - FAX   805-434-1098